ORIGINATE, MOTIVATE, INNOVATE

FOREWORD BY **SONYA RENEE TAYLOR**

SHELLY *Omi* BELL

CEO OF BLACK GIRL VENTURES

ORIGINATE, MOTIVATE, INNOVATE

7 STEPS FOR **BUILDING** A

Billion Dollar

NETWORK

WILEY

For general information on our other products and services or for technical support, please contact our Customer Care Department within the United States at (800) 762-2974, outside the United States at (317) 572-3993 or fax (317) 572-4002.

Wiley also publishes its books in a variety of electronic formats. Some content that appears in print may not be available in electronic formats. For more information about Wiley products, visit our web site at www.wiley.com.

Library of Congress Cataloging-in-Publication Data is Available:

ISBN 9781119900542 (Cloth)
ISBN 9781119900559 (ePub)
ISBN 9781119900566 (ePDF)

Cover design: Paul McCarthy
Cover photograph: Courtesy of the author

SKY10044703_032123

"Entrepreneurship is a boxing match, we the women know how to stay light on our feet."

—*Omi*

Contents

Foreword

A Treasure Among Us

I met Omíládé at an open mic night poetry event in Washington, DC, in 2009. In a room packed full of DC artists and Black bohemians Omí was a beaming poetry newbie. In true Omí fashion, after watching my 30-minute performance she came bounding up to me after the event and asked if I would be her poetry mentor. I was taken aback and simultaneously flattered. Her request felt above my pay grade—after all, I was still a broke poet late on her rent and cell phone bill. Nothing in me felt ready to mentor anyone, but I was compelled by her sheer exuberance and commitment to growth. Even then, Omí knew how to grow others while growing herself. What started off as a mentorship quickly grew into a friendship and relationship of reciprocity. Omí had endless skills and gifts I was in desperate need of. These myriad talents were in part developed by her wanderlust and epic curiosity, which took her from interest to interest like a hummingbird in search of the sweetest nectar. It was evident from early on that Omí understood how to gather and activate resources. She could see opportunity and all the disparate threads that needed to be woven together to stitch opportunity into a quilt, a tangible thing of utility and comfort.

In the mid-00s as two struggling young women, the glue of our relationship was a love of poetry and language and our shared hunger for community. We both knew community was our wealth and our bounty. We understood that the keys to the rooms we most desperately wanted to enter and the spaces that most desperately needed our presence lie in the collective. It was in community that we grew beyond ourselves and beyond the flimsy tropes society had pigeonholed us into. Today, Omí has taken that earned wisdom, that innate knowing and catalyzed it into a multimillion-dollar company and a billion-dollar network. She has used the riches of community to not only build her vision and empire but to create a network of women of color wealth holders around the country.

More than a decade later Omí is offering in this book the secret to what she has been building for as long as I have known her. She is offering the recipe of how authenticity, tenacity, and community can change our networks, our net worth, and our world. Omí and I have been blessed to see our fledgling visions grow into material success. We have birthed companies and hired employees, we have written books and sat among some of the most influential people in society. We are many moons away from two broke poets in a DC apartment rehearsing poems, but one thing has remained true. We have stayed in community because we know it is the most sustainable wealth we could build. And that knowledge alone is absolutely worth a billion dollars.

Sonya Renee Taylor

New York Times bestselling author and founder of *The Body Is Not an Apology*

Introduction

You picked this book up because you are on a journey. You are contemplating your next moves. You are reconsidering what society has told you that you can be. You are exactly where I was at the end of 2015. In the familiar Disney story *Cinderella*, a fairy godmother appears at a moment that Cinderella is feeling hopeless. The fairy godmother doesn't give Cinderella magic. She pulls the magic out of her with a few pumpkins, a new dress, and a carriage. She lifted Cinderella's belief lid and showed her what was possible. That is why you picked up this book. Now is the time for you to level up, and the good news is you've found the right resource to do it. Are you ready to go inside the rooms with high-powered CEOs of some of the world's most well-known brands? I hope so because I'm ready to take you there. Which is exactly what I will do. More importantly, you'll finish with the mindset shifts, tools, and tactics you need to succeed in the world of venture capital. You'll finish this book understanding the strategies needed to access capital for your business in a white male–dominated ecosystem. I've spent the last several years disrupting the world of venture capital as a Black woman and showing others how to implement successful strategies that lead to thriving businesses.

The May 25, 2020, murder of George Floyd by a Minneapolis police officer did more than intensify the call for criminal justice reform. It ushered in a new kind of awakening in the United States that rippled across the world. Global corporations began asking new questions about diversity, inclusion, and equity.

PayPal, Visa, TikTok, The NBA Foundation, TowerBrook Capital Partners, Johnnie Walker, the Amazon Alexa Fund, Omaze, and Rare Beauty Brands—to name a few—have reached out to Black Girl Ventures Foundation to understand how they can support the work we do to create access to capital for Black and Brown communities. I've been in rooms with many CEOs of those same companies, and some have even funded Black Girl Ventures. Women entrepreneurs are looking for a way into the venture capital arena, and I am here to lead the way. I know you want to know how to pioneer your path to capital. My book will help you do that. I revolutionized this space, and now I am here to testify.

People often ask me which is more novel, being Black or being a woman in the mostly white male space of venture capital. That question has me contemplating my journey up to this point in my life. I've never been a good employee. Either I was fired for asking too many questions, or I resigned because I was bored. As a result, I felt irresponsible because I couldn't keep a job. I changed my mind about what I was doing every three months. I asked myself: *What is my problem?* I wondered, did I lack focus, was I missing something, or missing out on something? But in 2016, I began to ask myself different questions. That year, the research said Black women started businesses at six times the national average yet received less than 1 percent of venture capital. I decided to poke at the boundaries of those limits to see what I could do.

I launched Black Girl Ventures Foundation (BGV), originally conceived as a competition pitch event called Black Girl Vision. For the first event, we charged a small entry fee, which was used to cover costs and to fund the award to the competition's winner. I created a Meetup.com event, and within seven days a couple of hundred members joined. Filling an event posted on Meetup.com held at a stranger's private home is not a common occurrence. But people came, not just once but repeatedly over a period of a year, and they were thoroughly engaged.

We branched out to partner with coworking spaces and eventually with Google to hold pitch events at Google offices around the country. I knew at that moment that I had come upon an idea that people wanted.

At the launch of the Black Girl Ventures Foundation, everybody assumed that venture capital funding happened in one way. It had to come directly from a funding entity—like a foundation, an investment firm, or a very wealthy single angel investor—to a founder. If an entrepreneur obtained funding from a group of separate individuals, it was known as crowdfunding, and the source of capital primarily included a local network of people the founder knew.

I have a simple goal. I not only want to share what I've learned on my entrepreneurial journey to success, but I also want to convey that my formula for achieving success may not work for you. You can, and you *should*, create your formula for making your "it" work for you.

I'm just so over the noise of society telling women and people of color what we can and cannot do. I want to say—in the clearest way—mute all the noise of other people telling you what is possible and what is not. Just focus on creating a truly unique process with your authentic story and distinctive way of approaching what you do, prioritize building substantial relationships, and then do everything your own way. Period. Your way is *the* way for you. This mindset is important because countless crucial inventions in every field—from technology to medicine—would never have been discovered if the architects of those ideas had listened to the conventional wisdom of their day.

If you can see yourself doing it—whatever "it" may be for you— you *can* do it! Be undeniable. Question, and at the same time, poke at and experiment with preconceived notions imposed on you by people, systems, ideas, and even history. The person who says, "I can do it" and the person who says, "I can't" are both right.

The book you hold in your hands (or that you are listening to) is special. Other business books either miss, overlook, or underrepresent the obstacles that women of color face at the intersection of race and gender (and sometimes sexuality) in the mostly white heterosexual male world of venture capital. This book will not give you one prescribed process to achieve success. It will reveal how one Black woman venture capitalist broke through gender and color barriers to getting funded but also to demonstrate how you can think about funding differently and break through those barriers too.

This book will challenge you to see yourself differently, by asking and answering the question: "Who would you be, if you were uninterrupted?" Because of white supremacy and the model it puts in front of us, I needed to ask myself: *Have I inadvertently and unknowingly swapped the goal of being free with the goal to be white?* Throughout the pages of this book, I will ask you to see your authenticity as a system disruptor, and that is a good thing. If you want to convey your vision to the rest of us, you need to show up as you. Authenticity is the most efficient way to hack into any system that has been designed to keep you out, including patriarchy and white supremacy.

It is my belief that our efforts to integrate diversity and equity into venture capital are failing because we live at the intersections of multiple discriminatory power structures, which are ironically hidden inside of diversity schemes. I will take you inside high-powered rooms where the CEOs of large companies meet to strategize and exclude people like me. I will show you how I enter those rooms and use my voice to make changes within. This will be an emotional journey as well as an empowering one. I will push you to see that there is no one way to get venture capital funding for your business. Your power is not in what you do but in how you think. With Black Girl Ventures, I have demonstrated that the crowdfunding model could be used to raise funds from numerous individuals and channel that money to single founders. I positioned Black Girl Ventures—a business entity—like a single individual to accept funds as a conduit to founders, and inadvertently disrupted how venture capital works. I am looking forward to taking you on this ride.

This book is broken down into three sections: originate, motivate, and innovate. The first three chapters address authenticity as a system hack and how you can create space by leaning into your community. Building community as the foundation of your business model has the potential to explode your career to the next level. When I say originate, I mean make community the origin point or springboard for your business. This is crucial during this time of great change and rapid technological advances that make it easier for your people to find you. Section II is designed to light a fire under you so that you can lean into your purpose, activate your social capital, and engage in an appreciation for the people around you. Section III of this book will give you the tools and tactics to lean into the thing that makes your business special. I will challenge you to innovate by tapping into your intuition and finding the beauty of living at the intersection of multiple things.

The last chapter of this book, "Omi's Toolkit," will give you systems to incorporate into your business practices and operations so that you can create a business that empowers people's lives and so that you can live the life of your dreams, on your terms.

PART I

Originate

CHAPTER 1

The Power of Asking Questions

The reason that there's no such thing as a stupid question is because asking a question is the most powerful thing you can do. I am Omí Bell, the CEO of a multimillion-dollar nonprofit called Black Girl Ventures. I'm a system disruptor and business strategist who moves ideas to profit while empowering people to live more authentically. I've been able to help thousands of women gain access to financial and social capital by disrupting the entire venture capital ecosystem. We'll talk more about that later, but one thing you should know up front is that I ask the tough questions. And I will challenge you to ask tough questions of yourself as well. The tough questions that I ask in high-powered rooms full of CEOs that don't look like me are no different from the questions I ask myself.

By the time I was seventeen years old America had already given up on me. I'm supposed to be a statistic. My future was supposed to be a crapshoot, and my options were supposed to be nonexistent or limited at best. You aren't even supposed to be reading this book right now. At least that's what society would have you believe. I had my first child when I was seventeen and still in high school. As a single mom and with baby in tow, I graduated on time and went to North Carolina Agricultural and Technical State University in Greensboro, North Carolina. Junior year of college, I had my second child, delivering my baby only one month before final exams. I was a single mom with two small children before I was even able to legally drink alcohol. On hundreds, if not thousands of occasions throughout my life, I've asked myself, *What am I going to do now? How am I going to make this work?*

On a personal and societal level, I've always questioned why things are the way they are. Why must we do things the way we've always done them? Why can't we choose a different path or better yet, why can't we create the path that works for our own circumstances? As you'll learn, I chose the latter. For me, the answers to these questions are found in the innovative business model that I needed all those years ago. This book is going to take you on a journey where these questions and more will be answered. You'll learn how I went from a single mom on government assistance to an internationally known business owner and brand. Most importantly, you'll learn how to build, nurture, and activate your social capital so you too can build a multi-million-dollar business of your own.

It is no secret that although there has been some improvement over the last few decades, women are still paid less than men with similar work experience, and men are frequently promoted over women; women with children are hired less, while men with children are paid more, and successful women are viewed as less likable than successful men. These realities are compounded when you're a single mom and head of your household. Several factors contribute to these facts, but one overlooked aspect of ordinary sexism in the workplace is the gender dynamics when it comes to asking questions. A recent peer-reviewed academic study called "Men ask more questions than women at a scientific conference" found that men asked 1.8 times more questions at conferences than women. Gender differences in speaking up and participation in a classroom setting have been studied over several decades. Lack of participation in these settings is detrimental to women climbing the corporate ladder, especially in male-dominated fields. Reviews of published academic studies have also found that overall, women participate less often and with lower confidence in the classroom than men. I've seen this up close and personal from my days of teaching computer science to grade schoolers in Southeast, Washington,

DC. This might sound unimportant or of little consequence at first glance. However, consider this: everything we know in the world of science began with someone asking a question and then seeking the answer.

The truth is no one knows everything. I constantly ask questions of myself as well as the people around me in order to make the best decisions possible. As I've grown in entrepreneurship, I've found that the questions people ask me can be pivotal to my success in business. The most biased questions I've confronted have led to some of the most lucrative opportunities. At a minimum, biased questions have provided an opportunity for me to build out a strategy that works for a Black woman in a predominantly white and male space.

The strategic power of asking questions is not always about getting answers, it's about opening your mind and understanding different perspectives. Not only the different perspectives of those around us but also challenging our own beliefs, to fine-tune our own methods, assumptions, and worldview. It's about making your own opinions better through the process of listening and learning from others as well as yourself. This has been pivotal to my success as an entrepreneur building out an innovative business model for the way Black and Brown women access capital and social networks.

If you were a fly on the wall when I and my closest friends talk, you'd probably be astounded by the number of times I ask questions of myself mid-conversation. It's a mix between a two-person conversation and a monologue. It might go something like this:

Me: I think I'm wearing red to the cocktail party tonight.
Friend: That's cool. I'm going to wear black.

Me:	That's interesting. Why do people usually wear black to cocktail parties? Like, when did that become a thing?
Friend:	I don't know.
Me:	Well, why do I want to wear red to a party when most people will wear black too?
Friend:	It'll make you stand out. Probably a good idea for networking.
Me:	True. Still, though, I'm gonna go look up why people usually wear black to cocktail parties.

You might be getting dizzy just by the circular, seemingly nonsensical back-and-forth in that conversation, but that's me. I ask questions and a lot of them. I know for sure that it has been a driver of not only my success but also my creativity. I'm going to share some practical ways you can use the power of asking questions to strategize, negotiate, and level up your career or business aspirations.

When I talk about the power of asking questions, I am not only suggesting you question your attitudes, values, and beliefs, but I am also urging you to use shocking questions from others as a catalyst to create strategies and opportunities. That is what we will be focusing on: how to use biased questions to your advantage, how to use questions to creatively negotiate in the world of venture capital, and how questions can propel you forward or shut you out.

Girls at the age of four are the most curious; they ask on average 390 questions a day, according to the book *A More Beautiful Question: The Power of Inquiry to Spark Breakthrough Ideas* by Warren Berger. That is about 24 questions every hour of being awake. I am a mother of three kids, and I can remember my kids asking questions such as, "Why is water wet?" or "Is the roof on the house, the same as the ceiling in my room?" However, as we grow older we tend to stop asking questions. We also do not take the time to interrogate the questions asked of us in order to grow in our personal and professional lives. This is a big mistake, especially for women business owners. As you will learn in the pages ahead, there have been questions asked of me that have led to major wins for Black Girl Ventures.

Questions are especially valuable in networking situations where you do not know anyone. I know for sure that the one thing people like to do is talk about themselves. From the richest person in the world to the poorest person in the world, everyone wants space and permission to talk about themselves. Asking people questions permit them to talk about themselves to you. Use this to your advantage and lean into being inquisitive, even when it might feel uncomfortable. Equipped with the knowledge in this chapter you will have the tools to become better in a room full of high-powered CEOs, become a better negotiator, and become a better business strategist.

Inside Rooms with Star Power

During the process of writing this book, a client asked me if I ever feel nervous when I am in rooms with other CEOs of major corporations or investors from Fortune 500 companies. My response was this: "Yes, I feel nervous like anyone else would, especially being the only one or one of the few Black women in these rooms." When my client asked me how I overcome this fear I told her that I've trained myself to focus on what I have in common with people. Additionally, I remind myself why I was invited to the room in the first place. Going into situations where you might feel nervous or intimidated is something every woman of color will experience in the financial capital industry as you climb the ladder and get more and more access. I remember being invited for the first time to a yearly networking event for companies that have a certain profit margin. This was my first time being invited to this particular event, and I remember going back and forth on what I was going to wear. I spent so much time trying to figure out what to wear to this event that a good friend of mine hit the pause button for me. She said, "Look, you're nervous, but there isn't anything to be nervous about. You already got invited. You're going to be in the room, so what difference does what you wear make?" She was right, and that's why whenever I start to feel what we call impostor syndrome kick in, I remind myself of all the wins and accomplishments I've amassed. You have to activate positive self-talk when you start to feel as if you shouldn't be in certain environments that signify status. You deserve to be there; otherwise, you wouldn't be invited in the first place. The next time you feel nervous or intimidated in a room full of investors or star power, take a moment to engage in positive self-talk, reminding yourself of all of the wins that led to this moment. That is what I did then, and that is what I do now, should I start to doubt myself. Now the question is, how do you work the room with people whom you look up to or feel intimidated by? The answer to this question is to focus on finding commonality between yourself and the person(s) you're talking to.

Once you find commonality with people who are intimidating or simply different from you, you can ease some of the fear and anxiety around any situation. The way you find commonality in those rooms is by asking questions aimed at finding something you can unite around. At this yearly networking event that

I had been invited to for the first time, I had the pleasure of sitting next to the CEO of Clear at the time, Caryn Seidman-Becker. At first, I was so nervous about this. Even though the event was very laid back and relaxed, I was super-nervous to actually not only be in a room with her but to be sitting right next to her. Caryn Seidman-Becker is co-founder and CEO of Clear, which uses identification technology for security checkpoints at airports and stadiums. She brought Clear into a 4.5-billion-dollar IPO (initial public offering). After hearing her talk, she mentioned that her father went to Howard University. This was an in for me to bring out something we had in common. I told her that I went to North Carolina Agricultural and Technical State University, which is also an HBCU. Once we bonded over something that we could unite around, I was then able to joke with her about the food at the event. She was totally relaxed. I was the one with the anxiety. We both agreed that the food wasn't that great. That gave us something to laugh about. After that, I could ease my nerves a bit. Uniting around things in situations like this is a way to remind yourself that even though someone might be further along on their journey, they are people just like you. They have some of the same fears, reactions, and shortcomings. I believe you can unite over something with everyone you might want to work with or establish a relationship within the business world. You just have to ask the right questions to find out what those commonalities are. On your journey, the next time you're in a room that is intimidating or bringing up feelings of inadequacy, remind yourself of all the amazing achievements that got you there. Then, find the person that you want to talk to the most and ask them a question. It could be as simple as saying, "I like your dress. Where did you get it?" or "I was thinking about getting the bulgogi as well. How is it?" You'd be surprised what these simple questions can lead to and how they can make you feel right at home with the people you look up to the most. You got invited. You are supposed to be there.

Business Strategy and Biased Questions

While we will come back to an approach called "design thinking" as a form of disruption later in this book, here it is useful to focus on how design thinking generates new ideas by asking questions. Design thinking is an iterative process where you start by asking the right question, then you do research, make observations, come up with ideas, and finally create prototypes of those ideas. It can be applied to any problem or situation where you want to create something new. Design thinking is an approach to generating creative insights about a particular problem. In the case of Black Girl Ventures, I created a business model that has become a prototype worldwide for organizations to provide access to capital to segments of the population that have historically been excluded. While on my journey I didn't know anything about design thinking or using the process of design thinking to create a new business model, looking back, the stages of design thinking are similar to my process. Black Girl Ventures, the social enterprise, has raised capital for over 500 Black- and Brown-owned businesses across 13 countries in under five years. My business model is atypical of the traditional ways the industry thinks about accessing capital and influential networks. Both of these are needed for Black and Brown women to be successful business owners. As of right now, $85 billion was invested by venture capitalists last year, yet women only received 2.2% of that investment. Black women only received 0.2% of this investment, totaling $3,740,000. When I had my first major fundraising meeting I was asked a jarring question to which I had a visceral and emotional response to, while remaining calm in the moment. I wouldn't realize it then, but that biased question layered with assumptions around race and gender was a catalyst to helping me create a new model that has disrupted the financial and social ecosystem of old. Here's what happened.

The first major fundraising meeting for Black Girl Ventures Foundation I secured was with a venture capitalist at a Fortune 500 company. I was nervous going into the meeting and wasn't quite sure what to expect. I didn't know the things I know now. I didn't have Black Girl Venture impact stats or even much social proof yet. I didn't know the different ways you approach different types of companies when fundraising or even how to articulate the larger vision of Black Girl Ventures. I was at the very beginning of my journey when I landed this meeting, and while I was seeing the impact through the BGV pitch competitions that I had done over the first two years, I didn't necessarily know how to package and pitch it to a potential investor. All I knew was that Black and Brown women were not getting access to capital, and I had struggled to get funding with my t-shirt print company, Ms. Print USA. I was still a bit wet behind the ears as I figured, maybe women of the past just haven't asked or haven't been in the right rooms. I did not yet understand the complex nature and disconnect between business ownership, fundraising, and investors. However, the complexities were made clear at this particular meeting.

During the meeting, I was giving my best pitch, or at least the best pitch I could at that time. At this point, I had funded nearly 40 women through the BGV pitch competitions. After detailing the work BGV had done up to that point the voice on the other end of the phone asked, "Why would I fund you? I don't do D&I [diversity and inclusion]. And we already have a group of women that we're funding." The brashness of his tone was severe. I had an immediate and uncontrollable reaction. I started speaking fast, as my heart rate accelerated, and my mind grappled for validation. I didn't feel comfortable enough to say, "Yeah, but you're funding groups that are all white. The women's group you're funding doesn't reflect the city you're in." Instead, I just kept talking about why BGV was great: "Well, we're doing this…," "We're funding people…," "We're getting…" It didn't matter what I said. His decision was made before he showed up to that meeting, and I didn't have the language to challenge him or change his mind. I left that call feeling like "I suck at this. I'm never going to be able to raise money. This is terrible."

While the question he asked is undoubtedly laced with multiple levels of bias, it is not an uncommon question for an organization that is run by a Black person serving Black and Brown people. If you're a Black or Brown business owner raising money, you may have unfortunately been asked a version of this question yourself. Is it an unfair question? Yes. However, here's what I learned from that question that propelled me to the next level of strategizing and ultimately winning. No, I never received funding from that Fortune 500 company, but today I receive so many emails from Fortune 500 companies looking to support BGV, I can't even respond to all of them in one day's work. That's what I mean by winning, and here's what that first investor call taught me. The question, *"Why would I fund you? I don't do D&I. And we already have a group of women that we're funding"* meant a few different things that had nothing to do with me. For one, I now understand after years of working in this field that the person you're pitching your business to likely has to answer to someone else. And that someone else is going to ask those same questions of them. More importantly, the man on the other end of the phone had already put me in the DEI box because of who I was and whom I served. This was 2017–2018, and while today I will fully embrace being thrown into the DEI box if it means I will get funding that will help Black and Brown women, back then I feared being thrown into that box. I didn't want to be considered the "Black company" or the "Black thing." I had a limited, misinformed view of the world of venture capital and how raising money works. Today I understand and I want you to understand that all money is green and all money builds relationships. Whether a company is funding you out of the DEI earmarked fund or some other line item isn't as important as raising money to grow your business. All business, whether nonprofit or for-profit, needs funding, and sometimes our limiting beliefs get in the way of that funding. I am not saying his question was appropriate, and trust me, I wish we didn't get categorized as a Black-owned business in this way, but the way the system is set up, we need to be able to capitalize on and understand the nature of the financial ecosystem beast. After that meeting I implemented a plan to be able to answer the question "Why should I fund you?" but it also motivated me even more to crack the code of understanding how Black and Brown women–led businesses could access capital and access networks that lead to more capital. I could have been defeated by his question. I could have simply taken my ball and gone home. However, I didn't. Instead, I studied his response, found the lesson in it, and started to refine my process. The takeaway here is that there are times that blatantly racist or sexist questions or biased questions can be a shocker, but what we learn from those questions, especially in the business world, can be a catalyst to take your business to the next level. So while we continue to disrupt and change the system, we can simultaneously find ways to benefit and grow from how it currently operates.

Something similar happened again around 2017–2018, again in the early years of building BGV. This time it wasn't in a formal setting with a potential investor, it was actually on a dating app called Bumble. I was on the dating app, looking for dates, and I swiped right on a guy that happened to be white. Let's call him Jack for the sake of this story. Jack swiped right on me as well, meaning we both liked each other based on the profiles we saw of one another. At least we both presumably liked each other. On Bumble, women have to make the first move. So I sent him a nice message introducing myself. To my surprise, he responded, but that wasn't the surprising part. Jack's first message to me was, "Oh, well, if I started a company called White Male Ventures, you would go ape shit?" and my response to him was, "No, that would be venture capital. Have you seen who's getting it?" From there Jack said some other rude things that aren't even worth mentioning. He deleted the thread, but not before I could get a screenshot of the conversation. I was floored by this exchange, not because I don't know that angry, racist people exist, but because I was not expecting to have this sort of exchange on a dating app with a stranger. I had so many questions. Did he swipe right on me just to have the ability to say something racist? I called a few of my friends to tell them what happened. Even though I had talked through it with several friends, I just couldn't shake that conversation. The situation kept replaying in my mind, so I decided to take it to another platform. That platform was Medium. Medium is like a hybrid between a blog and social journalism where amateur and professional writers alike can write articles, share thoughts, and engage with people. Medium is a source of original articles from a huge variety of people, including writers, poets, and artists from around the world. Some people find that Medium is a great place to share original articles and go viral since it's a huge blogging platform.

Instead of having an emotional response toward Jack, I decided to use Medium to write an article about what happened on Bumble. In the article I didn't just talk about the exchange I had with Jack, I also used it as a tool to talk about what Black Girl Ventures was doing in the venture capital space and the vision of the world I'd like to see as a Black-owned company focusing on funding women. In the article, I listed other women's organizations that were doing great work to support women, and then I pushed it to Twitter. I didn't think twice about it after the publication. However, after 24 hours or so, I noticed that the article was getting some traction. Bumble tweeted me back about it. At first, I didn't even look at the tweet from Bumble. Something was just telling me to look at the post, so I did. It was one of the content editors for Bumble. She apologized for my experience, which was standard, but she also did something else. She said, "We love what you're doing" and asked that I send her a direct message. I ended up on an email exchange with the company and learned that Bumble is a woman-led organization. They wanted to see how they could get involved with Black Girl Ventures. They were asking me questions such as, "Can we sponsor a pitch competition?" and "Can we see if we can offer mentors?" They told me that the ball was in my court on this potential collaboration. At this point, I was almost in tears, if I'm being honest. This was so early in the building phase of Black Girl Ventures that I was still learning how to talk to potential corporate sponsors. I still feel like I am bombing on calls with potential investors. I'm defining and redefining the core vision and goals of Black Girl

Ventures so I can articulate it perfectly to larger organizations. And here, a major organization was asking how they could work with me. It was surreal.

At this time in my journey to building this movement, I was constantly figuring out and pressing for corporate sponsors. At this point, I was making frequent trips to the chamber of commerce trying to learn how money moves and changes hands. Trying to understand why it was so hard for me and other Black and Brown entrepreneurs to get start-up funds. I was engaging with employee resource groups because I had learned that being on the internal calendars of multi-million-dollar companies and being shared internally was a good strategy to get funded. This meant activating Black and Brown employees at larger corporations in order to create a community that they felt a part of. Which in turn would allow my name and business to be mentioned in rooms that I was not privy to or people I could not get close to at the time. Bumble was a well-branded company with international recognition, and they were asking me how they could work with me. The ball was in my court. All from a racist question on a dating app. It wasn't the question in and of itself that led to this partnership, it was what I was turning that question into that made all the difference. I knew that if we could just start with one great corporate sponsor, we could push Black Girl Ventures in some different directions in terms of improving our success rate with partnerships, networking, and strong relationships with well-established brands. In thinking about how Black Girl Ventures could work with Bumble, I didn't want to be shortsighted. I saw this as an opportunity to do some amazing things at the moment but to also have a long-term mutually beneficial relationship with them. Partnerships, even at the early stages of business, are not just what other companies can do for you. It is also about the value you can add to those organizations. And you can add value. Bumble ended up being one of Black Girl Ventures' first major sponsors. Initially, they sponsored three pitch competitions, which gave us just the push we needed at the time. They sponsored pitch competitions in Chicago, Atlanta, and Washington, DC. In addition, Bumble has a Bumble Bizz side. On the app, you can look for people you want to date, but you can also look for friends or other professionals to connect with. Black Girl Ventures was sponsored by Bumble Bizz, and the cool thing about working with them was that people could find each other at the actual Black Girl Ventures events by using their proximity. So they would log into the Bumble Bizz app and then actually connect with people in the room at the pitch competition. This is a great example of how the partnership was mutually beneficial. Sometimes as early-stage entrepreneurs we are asking others for help with things, but we are not finding ways to give value to those people or organizations. When networking or exploring collaboration avenues, instead of asking, "How can XYZ company help me," ask yourself, "How can my company add value or help XYZ?" And frame your ask or lead into a conversation in that way. In this case, it was a mean-spirited biased question that led me to strategize around leveraging that experience and turning it into a winnable moment for my business. Not only can questions become a catalyst to something greater as was the case with Bumble, but they are also effective in negotiations of any kind. Ultimately, Bumble granted us $20,000, advised my staff on marketing as I built out a strong marketing team, and we became a referring partner for the Bumble Fund, which was designed to fund innovations founded by women. That's called a win-win!

Become a Better Negotiator

In January 2021, Nike, Inc., announced an economic empowerment partnership with Black Girl Ventures. Nike was looking to expand its Black community commitment by supporting organizations focused on social justice, education, and economic opportunity. And what better way to do that than to support an organization focusing on helping Black and Brown women entrepreneurs gain access to capital? Nike made a $500,000 investment in Black Girl Ventures, along with investing in other companies such as Black Girls CODE, NAACP Empowerment Programs, and the NAACP Legal Defense and Educational Fund, Inc., the previous year. What's useful here is how this partnership with Nike came about and how I used the power of questions to strategically negotiate the terms of the partnership.

The quality of the questions you ask in a negotiation situation will determine the quality of the answers you get as well as the quality of the results you get. It is very tempting to just accept the first offer someone presents to you, especially when you are in the early stage of business or when you do not feel you have the financial leverage to negotiate for what might be in your best interest. Whether it's a great job opportunity or a funding opportunity, everyone can relate to the feeling of not wanting to rock the boat or ask for what you want. Although I realize this is easier said than done, one thing I want you to take away from my partnership with Nike is that from the outset I was not afraid to think outside the box and ask them questions that gave me insight into how I could best leverage the partnership.

I have always practiced using my question muscle. When I first started my entrepreneurship journey running Ms. Print

USA, it was asking bold questions in crowded rooms that got me access to places such as Google Digital and large vending opportunities with major corporations. We'll come back to the Google Digital program and how that led to early success for my first company, Ms. Print USA, as well as the early days of Black Girl Ventures.

Getting buy-in from investors is about aligning your objectives with another company's objectives. If you go into a potential funding meeting with the only goal being to execute a flawless pitch, then you're missing a large part of what actually needs to happen to get funded. The very first thing you want to know when you're in the initial stages of working with another organization is what their objectives are. What would be a win for them? What segment of the population are they trying to reach? You need to know the answers to these questions as early as possible. And by early, I mean before you even go into a detailed pitch of your business. You want your pitch to show that your objectives overlap with theirs. You can't do this if you don't know up front what the other parties' objectives are. With that said, you also have to realize that sometimes you might need to walk away from funding opportunities if the partner company doesn't align with your values, mission, and goals. When Nike first approached me to discuss Black Girl Ventures, I didn't think much of it. I wasn't thinking they would fund Black Girl Ventures at all. Their initial communication to me was that they wanted to set up an informational call to hear more about the great work we were doing. They made it clear that they were not prepped to talk about grant funding but just a good connection point to a great organization. So, initially, I had no expectations of funding from Nike. Even though I had no expectations of funding, by this time I had learned how to talk to different types of potential funders, and we were getting organizations calling daily to potentially fund Black Girl Ventures. Part of the upswing in funding was that I was getting better at the business, I now had a team and a great board chair, but also George Floyd was murdered. On May 25, 2020, George Floyd, a 46-year-old Black man, was murdered in Minneapolis by then Officer Derek Chauvin. His murder was filmed and broadcast around the world via social media. It garnered major news coverage. There was widespread outrage, and as a result many companies made it a priority to combat institutional racism by making a commitment to Black-owned businesses. I was getting calls and emails from companies daily, and when I would show up to meetings people would have already read up about Black Girl Ventures. This was new for me. Previously I would have to spend time explaining the goals and mission of the organization and why we existed. Now, people were coming into meetings with us, having already done the leg work of learning about who we were and what we did. This made raising capital much easier. Even with Nike, my team had reached out to them via email about a year or year and a half earlier, and we never heard back. However, now Nike was reaching out to us to learn more. One thing I've learned is that you have to come to business meetings with your own questions as this will give you leverage to make a better pitch. While you're going to pitch your company and share your story during the meeting, it's critical to come with your own questions. That way, you can tailor your pitch and position your company for funding in real time but also in subsequent meetings. While I didn't expect funding from Nike, we had a few calls, and I began to realize on the second call that they did indeed want to work with us in some way. So during my second call with Nike, I asked the following questions: *How do we create a win-win? What would be a win for Nike?* This question is a power move because it is your moment to get an organization to tell you the core of what they really want. Then you can use that information to further drill down on the reason they should support you. I was asking for an understanding of how Nike wanted to engage with Black Girl Ventures. Being able to ask these types of questions is a mindset shift that you must make now, no matter where you are in your journey. As a young entrepreneur, I would have never thought to ask these types of questions because I was so in need of the money that I would just assume that I was there to answer questions and make the pitch. I wouldn't own my own power. I am here to tell you to own your power. When a company invests in you, it is a mutual relationship and you will get more mileage out of that relationship when you understand what the investor's goals are beyond just writing you a check. Understanding their goals will allow you to continue to speak their language so both organizations can benefit over the long haul, as opposed to a one-off funding event. You want continuity investors, and the way to do that is to find out early on what they are looking for in terms of their objectives. When you stand in your own power, you're not afraid to ask questions. You don't think your questions are going to turn someone off. You are not operating from a place of scarcity or fear. Money will come more easily when you operate from a place of power, as opposed to a place of desperation. As a small company in conversations with a large corporation and brand such as Nike, you naturally assume that Nike doesn't need anything from you. However, Nike wanted to work with community builders. Community builders drive stakeholder engagement. At that moment, I didn't recognize myself as driving stakeholder engagement. All I knew was that everyone was looking to give Black people money, and here I was on a call with Nike. By asking them what a win would look like for them, it empowered me to understand how my company actually was valuable to them. Once I learned that

Nike was looking for community builders and a win for them was to align with a great story, a charismatic leader, and a great organization connected to the economic development of Black and Brown people, I saw that our objectives aligned perfectly. I now understood how to better position Black Girl Ventures, but I was also confident that we aligned with what they were trying to do. Great story, a charismatic leader, and a great organization that was good at execution. Black Girl Ventures was all three, and I could prove it. By this time in my life as a businesswoman, I understood that meetings with potential funders were like dating. At the end of a meeting, you can tell whether someone is feeling you or not. You can tell whether they want to work with you. I knew they were feeling me. Nike would go on to invest $500,000 in Black Girl Ventures. Even though at this time, Black Girl Ventures had been receiving $3 to $4 million in funding from various sources, Nike gave us the largest single investment made by one company at that time. I would then go on to use the storytelling piece that was important to Nike to think outside of the box about what I would use the funding for. Storytelling was Nike's thing, but it was also mine. From my days on the poetry scene to the head of two organizations, I had long honed my ability to tell stories. Now I had a vehicle to do so on a large scale. I wasn't going to simply have an average relationship with Nike or do something average with the funding. I wanted to do something great, and I wanted to have a long-term relationship with Nike. This is where resisting average relationships with yourself and others comes into play. Going forward, we'll talk about how I used out-of-the-box thinking to further leverage the utility of the funding and how relationships were the key to a successful mutually beneficial partnership.

CHAPTER 2

Create S.P.A.C.E.

"Fail–Safe" Business Framework

The irony is that nothing about my life has been fail-safe. I have failed repeatedly. I've also always found a way to figure it out. As a single mom, you have no choice. If you don't figure out how to make it work, no one is going to do it for you. Being a single mom doesn't mean you don't have a community of people to support you, and it doesn't mean you can't create the community support you need. That's what building something that is fail-safe means. It means that independent doesn't mean alone. In Chapter 1, I mentioned going on government assistance, and I'd like to come back to that here. The average person has a really jacked-up perception of welfare or government assistance and the people on it. There is no shortage of nasty names, myths, and utterances about "those people" on welfare. I was one of "those people." Here's the thing, government assistance was a part of my journey to figuring it out. I wasn't just sitting around collecting a check and pushing out babies. Imagine going to the grocery store with your two-year-old and five-year-old. The kids are energetic and animated. We all know that kids are their best selves in the grocery store. Something about the grocery store and small children is a recipe for disaster. After making it out of the store without forgetting your pocketbook, a bag of groceries, or something else unexpectedly tragic happening you pull up to the front of your house. The kids have fallen asleep, and for a moment you enjoy the silence and peace in the car, but that is quickly disrupted when you realize you also have a car full of groceries. To make matters worse, you live on the second floor of your apartment building. How are you supposed to get all of the groceries in the house and watch the kids by yourself? You feel hopeless. Imagine it. There is no one to call. No one can come right now to help you. For a moment the only thing you know how to do is cry. This scenario isn't a one-off. It's something I had to figure out on multiple occasions. Today my oldest children are grown and thriving. I am grateful that I have a chef to prepare my meals and do the grocery shopping. I can pay people to be on my team. To manage the things I had to do on my own for so long. When I was on government assistance I always had a job. I cooked homemade meals for my kids. I worked side hustles before apps made it easy to find customers and build a business. I simply couldn't afford to raise two kids, have childcare, pay rent, buy food, and pay for food and shelter on the wages I was bringing in. I was, however, always motivated and innovative even when things felt hopeless all those years ago. One of the ways I thrived was through the community I built for myself and my family. I had strong family support as we'll discuss later on, but I also engaged other parents. I made friends at my kids', sporting events. I offered to babysit the kids of parents who played sports on the same teams as my kids. In return, they babysat when I needed it. In college, roommates who had become good friends helped me out with my children so that I could go to class and study. I've always understood that community is what it takes to thrive.

Researchers Gretchen Spreitzer and Christine Porath have actually studied how employees thrive. They've found that thriving employees are highly energized, but they also know how to avoid burnout. More surprising is that these same researchers discovered that people who belong to coworking spaces report levels of thriving that approach an average of six on a seven-point scale. Over the last decade, coworking spaces have exploded. In a recent *Harvard Business Review* article several coworking space founders discussed why those who work out of these types of office spaces thrive. The reasons range from more autonomy, to job control, and feelings of being a part of a community. I hold a special place in my heart for coworking spaces as early on in building Black Girl

Ventures, coworking spaces were some of the most accessible places to hold pitch competitions in various cities. They were easy to rent, relatively affordable, and they provided all the equipment that a traditional office would have. I remember one of my earliest pitch competitions in Philadelphia was held at a coworking space in Center City, with a skyline view. This was one of the first pitch competitions outside of my home base of the DMV (District of Columbia, Maryland, Virginia). What I view as important about the coworking space model is the community aspect. The entire foundation of a coworking space is built on the idea of community. You are a member, with perks and access to other members, and you can work independently or have access to others while in the space. All of these perks come back to the importance of community.

A report from the National Academies of Sciences, Engineering, and Medicine (NASEM) points out that more than one-third of adults aged 45 and older feel lonely, and nearly one-fourth of adults aged 65 and older are considered to be socially isolated. According to the Centers for Disease Control loneliness is the feeling of being alone, regardless of the amount of social contact. Social isolation is a lack of social connections. Social isolation can lead to loneliness in some people, while others can feel lonely without being socially isolated. At the time of writing this book a recent survey released by Cigna found that 71 percent of millennials and almost 79 percent of Gen Z respondents reported feeling lonely—a significantly greater proportion than other generations. Further, YouGov.com data show that one in five millennials report having no friends. With data like this, it's not surprising that despite the COVID-19 pandemic, demand for coworking spaces continues to grow. This isn't surprising to me. What it shows is that people want to feel a part of a community. And community is what I know best. It's the foundation of Black Girl Ventures and why my company, despite the pandemic, was able to thrive and grow even stronger coming out of the pandemic crisis. Yes, we had to pivot like every other business, but what we had on our side was an engaged community of women that still wanted to connect, that wanted to see their businesses thrive, and that still needed a space to congregate, virtually. We didn't have to suddenly start trying to find our tribe as a business due to the pandemic; we had already created Black Girl Ventures with community as the staple. This was a huge advantage for us, and I am here to teach you how to use community building as the foundation of a sustainable business model. Before I deep-dive into some of the ways my team leaned into community during the pandemic in order to build a bigger and better organization, I want to take a moment to talk about how I have come to instructively build community and why it shows up in every facet of my entrepreneurship journey and personal life.

I'm from Durham, North Carolina. Yes, I know what the best barbeque tastes like, and yes, North Carolina has the best biscuits. I had a very Black upbringing. My mom's side of the family and my dad's side of the family are very different and speak to different social classes. However, one thing is the same, both sides feel like home for me. That sense of belonging is where I learned to innately lean on my community, and it shows up in nearly everything I do or create. I got community from both sides. As for my mom's side of the family, her generation grew up on government assistance. However, it didn't feel that way. The projects simply felt like community. It didn't feel crime-ridden or dangerous, it felt like the family was all under the same roof, under the same conditions, living as a tight-knit working family. That's the experience they had, and that's how it felt.

There is a forgotten history around how the United States government segregated America through public policy that created and remains responsible for what we call "the projects." For decades some of the poorest people in the United States have lived in subsidized housing developments often known as the projects or the ghetto. These communities are the result of racist policies employed by the government. There are myriad reasons for this, including the New Deal's National Housing Act of 1934 enacted by Franklin D. Roosevelt. This and other housing programs of the 30s, 40s, and 50s were explicitly racist. The FHA had a manual, which explicitly said that it was risky to make mortgage loans in predominantly Black areas. So while the New Deal Housing Act promoted homeownership by providing federal backing of loans or guaranteed mortgages, from its inception, the FHA limited assistance to prospective white buyers (not Black buyers). As a result, Black people had a housing shortage coming out of the Great Depression, in which governmental policies funneled Black people into poorly constructed and underserved communities, or as we know them today, the projects. In addition to the FHA's racist policies and practices, federal housing projects from the 1930s onward were designed to keep Black Americans in neighborhoods with fewer education and job opportunities than white neighborhoods. At the same time, the government-sponsored Home Owners' Loan Corporation and the Federal Home Loan Bank Board used maps to deny lending and investment services to Black Americans—this, known as redlining.

On my dad's side of the family, my grandfather owned his own construction company. He built houses and helped build commercial buildings. He wanted to have his own and make his own money, in the same way his father, my great-grandfather, had done. That's how he was raised, and that entrepreneurship spirit was certainly passed down to me. Early on I heard the tales of entrepreneurship from someone who was making a living and living well, without clocking into a nine-to-five job. My grandfather created his own income, his own work, and was proud of that. He vowed, "I will never work for white folks." He lived to be 93 years old, and he never worked for "white folks." He re-created himself over and over again and then found ways to make a living from it. As desegregation evolved, the city of Durham, North Carolina, (my hometown) offered Black men an opportunity to work construction for the city. The appeal of benefits and higher pay caused my grandfather's workforce to dissipate. Instead of taking the same route, my grandfather pivoted to installing glass doors, then to creating a 100+ person mass choir that traveled the country, to finally launching his own church where he would pastor until he passed away. Due to my grandfather's grind, my dad's family was more upper middle class compared to my mom's side of the family. My dad never became an entrepreneur. In fact, he refused to take that path. However, entrepreneurship was in my DNA. I noticed stark differences in mentality based on socioeconomic status. There is a psychology to social class that you may or may not have recognized in your own familial situations. A research study out of the *British Journal of Social Psychology* found that "those who grow up in middle- or upper-class environments are likely to have more material and psychological resources available to them, and as a result have stronger beliefs about the extent to which they can shape their own social outcomes; by contrast, those who grow up in lower-class environments are likely to have fewer resources available to them, and as a result have weaker beliefs about their ability to control their outcomes." I saw similar patterns to this phenomenon growing up. For example, if my dad's family were to run out of medicine, they would share their medicine with the family member that needed it. They would share things like insulin. As opposed to my mom's side of the family, who would be more likely to ask you for a hundred dollars for basic bills but would never ask you to share medicine or to help them pay for their medicine. For my mom's side of the family, being communal was expected, but being collectively healthy was never really much of a conversation outside of an extreme focus on weight loss. On my dad's side of the family, money wasn't an issue, so they wouldn't ask for money; they would ask for exactly what they needed at the time. When you have the mentality that money will always be there or money will come to you, you tend to attract more money. However, when you have a scarcity mindset the thing you always want or are in search of is money, regardless of whether that is what you actually need at the time. It's a psychological shift that often separates those who can benefit from educational and occupational opportunities to improve their material circumstances, for example, and those who cannot or do not. And yet, regardless of the difference in mentalities both families valued each other, and family functions, on both sides, felt like community. Even through the toughest of times, I always felt a feeling of fellowship with the people around me. This feeling translates directly into the business model I created for Black Girl Ventures Foundation (BGV) and before that, Ms. Print USA, going all the way back to my days in the DMV, putting on poetry slam events. This brings me to the methodology I share with clients on creating a fail-safe business. Although a fail-safe business model or idea does not exist, I encourage any Black or Brown woman that I am coaching or advising to spend just as much time creating community as they do selling their product or service. If the foundation of your business is community, then you are as close to having a fail-safe business as you possibly can. Communities come with engaged people, language systems, ideologies, shared goals, vision, and things like loyalty and purpose—all keys to success for organizational leaders.

A while back, I was coaching a woman who ran a branding company. Her business was breaking even a little over a year in. She was having success selling a high-ticket coaching package, but she felt that in order to grow her business long term she needed to find a way to create a community. Her hunch was correct. She explained to me that delivering information to her clients felt more like she was speaking to an audience of people who were listeners, but not active participants. She reasoned that this would be a problem as she thought about growing her company long term. The first thing I pointed out to the client was that I've never thought of anybody watching or engaging in what I had to share as anything other than a community. I've never thought of people as simply an audience in the way she described. Even during my days as a teacher in Alexandria, Virginia, I felt in community with the students and families. My relationship-building sphere is this idea that strangers are just friends you haven't met yet. Anybody has the potential to be something other than what you initially met them as. That is my frame of reference. I wanted my client to understand that she needed a slight mental shift in the way she was even thinking about her customers, especially because she provided a service in which people worked one-on-one with her. She wasn't simply giving them information in a linear way; she was actually having a bidirectional conversation, and in essence, she was indeed already creating and engaging in community. However, she needed to be intentional beyond the one-to-one coaching to ensure the longevity of her business and move closer to a fail-safe business model. Once my client was able to make that mental shift, I then encouraged her to think about where her clients or those interacting with her brand go to gather. As someone who spent years performing poetry and organizing poetry events, I had practice in creating spaces. That is, making spaces gathering spots for like-minded people. That's why when the pandemic hit in March 2020, I was able to pivot quickly and seamlessly into the virtual sphere while maintaining the ability to create space for Black and Brown women business owners. I had an amazing copywriter and event organizer on staff already. The team immediately mobilized to increase things like Facebook and Instagram copy to create engaging content that provided the community with valuable information. Then we held regular virtual coworking sessions where the community would meet on Zoom to work together. We'd start the session by briefly discussing what each person was working on, and women could choose to participate in this portion at their own discretion. Then we'd sit on Zoom for hours working. As I reflect on that period of not just a deadly unknown virus but also the murder of George Floyd, it makes me emotional. During this time we didn't even know if it was safe to do things like go outside. I was in my apartment in Virginia, still doing my best to offer a space for these women and if I'm honest, a space for myself. Once you fully embrace the value of communities, you can transform any business into a space or social container, as I like to call it, to provide support, comradery, engagement, and commitment to your brand. Ultimately, how I create community also increases brand commitment, which in turn provides Black Girl Ventures both quantifiable and unquantifiable benefits.

What I want you to understand in terms of your own business model is that communities are powerful. They are a place where people can find support, advice, and inspiration. They are also an opportunity to develop new skills and widen their reach through mutually beneficial connections. Community members feel more connected and loyal to a thing when they share common interests, beliefs, or backgrounds among others. The sense of belonging often drives them to take a more active role in the community itself—whether that is volunteering or contributing in some other way. So for anyone facing a similar situation with their organization, I'd first sit down and think about where do or can your constituents gather. Is it virtual like Zoom or Skype? If so, put together a live webinar and allow the attendees to introduce themselves and network with one another after your presentation. Can they gather in person? Create a mastermind group where everyone in attendance can learn from one another and share ideas. Finding a way for your constituents to gather does not need to be setting up a super-elaborate event or spending thousands of dollars renting out an event space. Creating a social container for your organization where people can meet virtually or in person is the first step to allowing people to engage with others and with you, the business owner. A social container is an environment set up and programmed with attributes that add value to the people that will be a part of that space. It is creating positive tribal energy that gives people a sense of belonging over a sense of gathering. The key to creating successful social containers is to focus on creating a many-to-many group experience versus a one-to-many experience. In a many-to-many experience the community works with the community, which enhances the value of being a member of that community. In a one-to-many experience the community being built is reliant on the value added by one entity. Many-to-many experiences are more sustainable and scalable. Even digital ecosystems, such as websites, can utilize a community framework. You should think of your website as a center city when it comes to helping people navigate to the social containers you've built.

When you are thinking about creating your website, you want to make sure it is "sticky." That is, when people land on your website you want people to stay awhile. You want people to click around and find places they can go within and across your website. When someone on your website wants to take a train to another part of your digital ecosystem, they can click on a link to go find more people or resources that resonate with them. You design your city or website so that people marvel at the buildings, stop in a café with like-minded people, and feel at home. Your website can give people a chance to engage with you as well as with others visiting the site. That's what it means to have a social container. It's simply a vessel to allow engagement. Now that you have the basic foundation on how to begin to think about moving your existing business to a more community-centered organization, let's dive into the Black Girl Ventures business model methodology, which I have coined S.P.A.C.E. This will give you a system that you can employ to strengthen your business and create a business model based on community.

Back to my client that owned the branding company. She was sold on the idea of creating a social container or even multiple containers for her members to gather. From there I laid out the Black Girl Ventures business model methodology, S.P.A.C.E. The term "space" is fraught with tension for people of color, and the use of the acronym for the BGV business is by design, intentional. We need to change the narrative around taking up space and make a psychological shift to take up more space. Black and Brown women are often told to "take up less space." They are told to shrink themselves, to not take up too much space. This is a form of racism and sexism that is very common in the United States, and I have witnessed it in the venture capital world. We are often told to make ourselves smaller. The lack of space for our bodies is not a new phenomenon, but it has been happening for centuries. Black and Brown women have been told to be less loud, less talkative, and less visible to make room for other voices. But I want us to feel empowered to take up more space than ever before. "Taking up space" is a term used by Dr. Diandra Leslie-Pelecky in her book *The Space Tween* to describe the way that Black people are often asked or expected to take up less space than others. It's not just physical space in a room or on the street—it's emotional and mental spaces too. The question becomes, "How do you create the social container you want?" The answer is: create S.P.A.C.E. First, you need to consider the "S," which is *safety*.

The "S" in the S.P.A.C.E. Framework Is Safety

Safety means that people need to feel safe and secure in the social container you have created for them to gather. Safety is not only a part of how I think about my business model, but it is also my parenting style. For example, when you have a room for young kids to play in, the first thing you do is look at how the room is set up. You need to make sure there is safety for a child to operate within that room. For toddlers, you'd make sure there were no sharp objects. You'd make sure that things are positioned in a way that won't harm the child. You intentionally place or move things to avoid problems. That doesn't mean that every way that the child walks through the room, you go, "Wait a minute, don't do that." You set the social container up so that your child can feel free to play. When thinking about creating a social container for the members and constituents engaged with your brand, when people enter the space you want to provide them with the ability to engage with each other freely, in that same way. For my client with the branding company, I made her think deeply about the types of ways her members could gather but first think about what her target group needed to feel safe in a space. When people feel safe they will engage each other on their own. It will be organic. A place should feel safe for the people who enter it. This is because the environment influences our mood and behavior. It also impacts how we feel about ourselves and others around us. A place can make us feel more confident, less confident, emotionally drained, or energized.

A person's surroundings, their environment, can affect their mood in significant ways. This is one factor that determines whether a person feels comfortable enough to engage. You don't have a solid community unless people are engaging, which we will tackle in the next few pages as well. It's not just about the people in the space but the atmosphere and how intentional you are about creating a place designed for interaction. *How do you create an intentional atmosphere?* Great question! The first thing to think about is the location. When I ran my first pitch competition in Washington, DC, I held it at a home in Southeast, DC. Many people know Southeast, DC, for its crime rates or they may have heard of this part of DC as a more undesirable place to be—somewhere you don't go at night. However, as someone thinking about the vibe I wanted to create, this was the perfect geographical location to build a community. It felt like home. It did not feel pretentious or a place where we should feel self-conscious or unwanted. At the first event, my friends helped me set up and it was a small group of women who were all there with the same goals—to network, talk about their business ventures, and support each other. The social container was intentionally intimate. I had home-cooked food at the event, and instead of just going right into the pitch competition when the women arrived, I built in time for the women to network and talk. The beginning of the event was more like a mastermind where we exchanged ideas and created a beautiful atmosphere of support and engagement. I was right there with them learning and growing as well. I wasn't just the organizer or leader; I was an active participant in the experience. After you have decided on the social container in which people will meet and think genuinely about all the ways to make it safe in order to meet your goals of creating a community, you then need to make sure your social containers are predictable.

The "P" in the S.P.A.C.E. Framework Is Predictability

People need to know what to expect when they gather in the space or spaces you create for them. Predictability in business means consistency. Not only consistency in brand messaging and deliverables but the way you show up and the atmosphere you create. The way you create virtual and physical spaces for your tribe needs to be predictable. Every successful company is predictable. People feel comfortable when they know what to expect. Predictable brands are more likely to be successful than unpredictable ones. Predictability is a key factor in creating the right kind of customer experience. Companies should be predictable in order to create a positive customer experience and maintain their brand image. They should also be predictable to their employees, suppliers, and other stakeholders. There is a popular communication theory called uncertainty reduction theory (URT) by scholars Charles R. Berger and Richard J. Calabrese. URT says that the more you interact with someone, the less nervous you become because over time you have expectations about how the person will interact with you. When you first meet someone, you might be a little nervous because you are unable to predict how the person will receive you, respond, or behave. It's the same thing when someone comes to one of your first events. They are unsure of what the experience will be. However, if they like the experience one time and they come back to another one of your events, then they are expecting to have a similar or predictable experience. Think about your favorite dish at your favorite restaurant. You want it to taste the same every time. If you order your favorite dish and they have added or removed an ingredient and it tastes different, you will be disappointed. It's the same reaction people have when interacting with the different social containers you create for them. In terms of the physical or virtual space you create for people to gather, the experience needs to be consistent. That way they can trust you, and if they had a good experience, they are more likely to come to your next event and recommend your event to other like-minded people. Predictability is not inherently positive or negative. Predictability does not breed optimism; it creates a baseline of trust. This could be trust that a thing will happen or trust that it won't. Either way, predictability breeds trust. You will have to maintain an organization on which thing is best for you.

For Black Girl Ventures, as I went on with organizing and executing the pitch competitions a few years into the business, I began to use spaces at Google and coworking spaces in other cities. I was a long way from the days of doing events in a home in Southeast, DC, but the vibe was still the same. These concepts were still applied in order to stay consistent. Women who were there from the early days of the Black Girl Ventures competitions in Southeast, DC, and women who come to the events today tell me that while the venues are bigger and better, the energy is still the same. There is still networking, collaboration, development opportunities, and familiarity, just with better technology, video cameras, and more members of the community. I've never lost sight of the purpose, and being consistent in my purpose allows the events to remain predictable for the community I serve.

The "A" in the S.P.A.C.E. Framework Is Access

The "A" in "S.P.A.C.E." stands for *access*. Those people that you are engaging with and creating spaces for need to have access to you as well as others. You have to give people opportunities to engage with you. When you create something that's based on a one-to-one interaction, challenge yourself to think about other ways community members can engage with you and other members. Ask yourself, *Are you only setting up yourself to engage with them or are you allowing them to get what they need from you in different ways? What other ways can they access you?* Also, *what other ways can they freely engage with other people outside of the events you organize? What other ways do they have to commune?* You can build these communal spaces off your personality as well. This might look like membership sites, live group coaching at the same time every month, virtual coworking that you lead, engaging with those who interact with you on social media, or many other access points. Taking time out of your day, every day, to engage with the people who are asking you questions and commenting on your content online is crucial to maintaining an engaged community. Can you imagine posting content on Instagram and someone shares a personal story and I just hit them with a smile emoji or heart? You need to be purposeful around this concept of access. Access does not mean that you are available to all people at all times. It is being intentional about creating avenues outside of spaces to allow members to connect with you and others that like your brand.

The "C" in the S.P.A.C.E. Framework Is Collective

You also want to think about creating a collective of communal spaces, which is what the "C" in S.P.A.C.E. stands for, *collective*. By collective, I mean that you need to have more than one communal space as you grow your business. Your communal space could be a tight support circle of friends and a therapist, other entrepreneurs who understand your journey, coworking space, training cohort opportunities, etc. Your collective may look different from someone else's. Think long term about the multitude of ways you can create these social containers. That's why we created the Black Girl Ventures Change Agent fellowship. Aside from the pitch competitions, networking opportunities and events across various cities we needed another vehicle to help people engage. We needed a different type of communal space as we grew. The Change Agent Fellowship is a totally unique nine-month leadership skills development program created specifically to expand the capacity of early-stage Black and Brown entrepreneurs and ecosystem builders. The fellowship incubates Black and Brown women, identifying founders and ecosystem builders across multiple local ecosystems as a means to amplify women leaders and to create an "each one, teach one" model for growing the long-term entrepreneurial knowledge and sustainability of underrepresented founders. Black Girl Ventures cultivates local leaders, who in turn cultivate their community as a service to the greater good of creating equal opportunity to thrive at the intersection of being a Black and Brown woman and an entrepreneur.

As the collective of your spaces grows stronger and reaches more people, you will then have a business that has more resources to give back to your members. For example, the Change Agents fellowship comes with a $10k stipend, plus in-kind resources to help fellows grow their business. It also gives fellows access to the other communal spaces across the Black Girl Ventures brand. You can think big about the collective of spaces you create for your target members as your company grows stronger and moves closer to a fail-safe business model. This leads me to the "E" in this methodology, which is *engagement.*

The "E" in the S.P.A.C.E. Framework Is Engagement

A community isn't anything without engagement. While engagement is a thread throughout this entire methodology, it is imperative that your goal is engagement when you implement the ways in which you create space for your target members.

Engagement simply means giving people a way to participate. You want people to participate, instead of spectating. While you are taking the time to create the spaces, you want to be deliberate about multidirectional engagement opportunities for all types of personalities. When I was a computer science teacher, I understood that some students were excited to raise their hands and participate and others weren't. Some students were better writers or test-takers. Others were better performers or better at setting an example. Because of the various types of people that will be a part of your membership, you need to find ways to accommodate all types of personalities so that everyone has an opportunity to engage. Think about the numerous Facebook groups you are in. Some of them you might check regularly because people are posting, celebrating and discussing things. Others may have low communication, rare posts or maybe there are posts, but no one is commenting on the content. The latter has low engagement. The administration of that type of group has not curated or posted content that the members want to engage with. However, it's not just about the content. This is why this concept of S.P.A.C.E. is so powerful. The engagement will come if you have spent time creating safety, predictability, access, and a collective.

Looking back on the journey so far, I understand that the multiple business ventures and failed attempts before landing on Black Girl Ventures were all moving me closer to this business model that I know will help Black and Brown women create stronger, more fail-safe organizations. Is any idea or company fail-safe? I'd be lying if I said it is simple to create one. However, I know for sure that if you start to implement the S.P.A.C.E methodology that I and many of the founders I work with have implemented, you will move your business closer to withstanding the test of time. I didn't know I was creating a business model that would be a prototype for so many, but what I did know early on is that I needed to create a new way of doing things based on the data. Black and Brown women continue to be underfunded and left out of the world of venture capital as they build their businesses. Something new had to enter the scene, and that meant a new approach was needed. Previously in this book, I mentioned the approach of design thinking, which is all about creating successful services and products by solving problems using creativity and empathy. The design thinking approach is worth considering as you think about solving the complex problems your company will face and the challenging problems you are trying to fix as a business owner. Black Girl Ventures was trying to find a way to support more women in creating and sustaining companies in a world that leaves them out of the ecosystem of capital. As I look at my business model, I employed a design thinking approach to solving the problem I saw, which I believe will be useful to you.

Design thinkers use four steps in order to make their product or service successful: empathize, define, ideate, and prototype. This framework has been informative in helping me understand the methodology behind the Black Girl Ventures business model and why it works so well. The time I spent hustling and bustling trying to get Black Girl Ventures off the ground, I viscerally felt the pain of all the Black and Brown women trying to crack the funding code. All businesses, whether nonprofit or for-profit, need outside funding, yet Black and Brown women receive less than 2 percent of venture capital funds. The empathy I developed through experience and being in the same situation as so many of my Black and Brown counterparts has motivated me to find a new way of doing things. Through my community-based approach I have been able to interface with thousands of women, which has allowed me to develop a shared understanding of what our needs are. This has allowed me to define in no uncertain terms the problem that Black Girl Ventures was seeking to address, and I believe in this business as an achievable framework to move your business from where it is today to a solid business enterprise that will have longevity.

Here are the facts: Black women start businesses at six times the national average, yet 70% lack access to capital from friends and family. Black women are 13.7% of the population and 18% of low-wage earners. Black and Brown women receive less than 2% of venture capital and access loans at far higher interest rates. Minority-owned businesses spend 11% more than others on Federal contracting because they don't have connections. As I move forward I continue to generate solutions to address these harsh facts. The ever-changing needs Black and Brown women face in the entrepreneurship space are real. Sometimes it can be hard to keep up. At any given time in one's business, the needs of the organization will shift. Sometimes a business owner might not even be clear on what their business needs are or even worse, what they think they need might not be what will benefit them. However, beginning with a community mindset will never steer you wrong. That's why the collective of spaces Black Girl Ventures provides allows us to meet the needs of entrepreneurs at various stages on their journey. I am proud that Black Girl Ventures, through the S.P.A.C.E methodology, can be the protype from which your business can thrive by replicating the framework.

CHAPTER 3

Be Authentic and Build Your Brand

As I was writing this book I asked new and old friends if they feel like they've seen the softer, more feminine side of me or just the more hard-core, hard driving, less emotional, detached side of me. This question was on my mind because I was thinking about my brand, particularly across my social media accounts. My content is about educating women on the world of venture capital, sharing my wins, and helping Black and Brown business owners learn from my journey as a successful entrepreneur. It's also, of course, about using these platforms to create and engage my community. Friends that have known me personally for years as well as newer friends overwhelmingly told me that they predominantly view me as a "boss babe" or as being "hard-core." The people closest to me view me in the same way as those who only know me through my content online. They know me as a business owner on her grind that doesn't take smack from anyone and knows how to play with the big dogs. This aspect of me is conventionally viewed as masculine in our culture. But while the people closer to me have seen the softer, more vulnerable side, they can't see past my brand when I ask them how they view me. This is a testament to the success of the way I've built my brand. My brand is so strong and intentional that even people who personally know me view me through the lens of my brand persona. Even when my friends see me vulnerable or more conventionally feminine, my brand supersedes these experiences because it takes a different part of our brain to visualize something more nuanced and complicated. Within my brand persona are the aspects of me that I am positioning to the world, and those aspects are authentic to me. Building a business must include being intentional about your brand persona. A brand persona tells the story of who you are, forefronts the aspects of your personality that fit the mold of your story, and if done successfully, it is so strong that people feel as though they really know you. The trade-off to this is that the world doesn't get to see the other aspects of who you are unless you choose to let them see behind the curtain. This should be used to your advantage because building your brand means that you have room to grow your brand and rebrand down the line. There are certain aspects of who I am that are invisible to those who interact with my brand, and so I am associated with the brand persona that is public facing. There is a paradox to this invisibility that is important for women entrepreneurs to lean into while also understanding how building a brand works both publicly and personally. That's what this chapter will help you work through—invisibility as a major player in better understanding ourselves and the world around us as it relates to the intersection of authenticity and building a powerful brand.

The Invisibility Paradox

Who would you be if you were uninterrupted? The answer makes me think of Ruby Baptiste, a Black character on the popular HBO series *Lovecraft Country*, struggling with the interruptions of life and the currency of whiteness. Ruby says, "I don't know what is more difficult, being colored or being a woman. Most days I'm happy to be both, but the world keeps interrupting, and I am tired of being interrupted." The first step to becoming a part of a new network with people who have more knowledge or wealth than you is to see yourself differently—to see yourself as if you had not been interrupted.

That HBO episode opens with Ruby waking up in the house of William, the white man she had met and gone home with the night before. We watch as Ruby stretches her hands casually past her eyes. Then, startled at what she sees, she clumsily rushes to the mirror and reacts in horror: she's in a white woman's body. William explains what's going on as dark blue and black butterflies hover around the bed: "A butterfly lives a full life before it dies. Then a caterpillar emerges from the same cells, the essence of the butterfly, yet different. It's more." The magic potion that William had given Ruby mimics metamorphosis. In her new skin, Ruby goes out for a casual stroll for ice cream. Everybody she encounters is pleasant and accommodating. When she returns home, William asks why she hadn't spent any of the money he had left for her that morning.

"I enjoyed my entire day using the only currency that I needed—whiteness," Ruby responds.

I was struck by the audacity of that statement. As the episode continued, I was reminded of a type of rhythm of walls that people of color and women move through as we encounter all the messages from external places that say, "You can't," "You won't," "You look like this, so you can't do that."

A few years ago, one of the white actors from one of the Avengers movies tweeted something to this effect: "Black women have it so good because they can say everything they want to say and I can't." Of course, Black Twitter aggressively converged to annihilate her. The news exploded across the Internet.

But what she was trying to say, although admittedly ineloquently, was, "I don't have space to assert myself." From her vantage point, despite the inequities with centuries-old patterns of discrimination against Black people, at least Black people can be vocal about the injustices they experience. But she felt like she had no room to assert herself, to be bold, to be authentic, because she had to appease her own constraining environment of being a white *woman.*

Later in the *Lovecraft Country* episode, we discover that William is also a body double, for his sister Christina, a comment on the interruptions that white women experience in a world created for white men.

And then Christina poses the most powerful question I have ever heard. She says to Ruby, "You misunderstood William's invitation. It wasn't just to be white. It was an invitation to do whatever the f&^% you want." Christina holds up the magic potion to Ruby, asking "Who are you…really, uninterrupted?"

I replayed that question, over and over, because I needed to hear that message. I needed to ask myself: Because of white supremacy and the mold that it puts in front of us, *have I inadvertently and unknowingly swapped the goal to be free with a goal to be white?*

I was shaken emotionally. *How have I been interrupted?*

The answer came quickly: in multiple ways, all the time.

Like the times I've sat in meetings where a white woman made a suggestion that everybody thought was great, and I had literally just said the same thing, but the table said, "Oh, no, I don't think we should do that."

Or the times when a white woman was pegged as being annoying, and I was labeled angry for complaining about the same thing in the same way.

And all the times that I still have to think about my voice being too strong, and how I need to calm it down, make it lighter, and use more breath so that I don't intimidate people. I'm told, "Smile because that will help your words land the right way."

Each one of these micro-aggressions is an interruption, and in these situations those interruptions are invisible to those around us.

And so, when you ask yourself, *Who would I be if I were uninterrupted?* recognize this is one of those questions that could reshape your life.

When I'm uninterrupted, there's no disconnection between who I am and what I can do. I don't need to speak as much or overstate my ideas. I don't have to worry about finding just the right way to explain my ideas to an audience of funders who didn't have my same experiences. I'm not interrupted by what you do not want. I'm not interrupted by the change you don't want to happen.

When I'm uninterrupted, I only focus on the change I want to happen.

In 2020, I partnered with a credit card company and the Small Business Administration (SBA) to put together a panel for National Small Business Week. I contacted a Black woman who is known in the space to invite her to be a part of the panel. She enthusiastically said yes. However, once the customary vetting process occurred, it was discovered that she had appeared in an article that criticized the Paycheck Protection Program (PPP). As a result, she did not clear the vetting process and had to be uninvited. Nevertheless, the real reasons behind the renege on her invitation were invisible to her. While as Black and Brown people we know racism when we see it, sometimes there are other, invisible things behind the scenes that present us with a paradox. Unseen factors that may or may not have anything to do with our identity.

When I conveyed the news, her response was visceral but not unexpected. She strongly believed that the organizers did not want powerful Black women on the stage. In her defense, she said she was telling her truth about what happened with the PPP, and they didn't want her truth.

Her response prompted me to ask more questions, because I needed to know if the accusation accurately described the situation. After more conversations with my partners, I realized there was another power struggle happening that had nothing to do with us. The SBA and the Trump administration were squabbling, and the SBA couldn't afford to associate with anyone who presented even the slightest hint of negativity related to the PPP. The stakes were high; financial assistance to thousands of failing businesses around the country hinged on two powerful egos finding a way to work together.

That was the reality of the situation. I was struck by the difficulty I had conveying that message. It was hard to go back to the woman and say the decision not to bring you onto the panel isn't because you're Black. It isn't because you're powerful. It isn't because you didn't deserve to say what you wanted to say. You absolutely deserve to say what you want to say.

To go back to her with that message ran the risk of sounding like I was conceding to systemic racism buried deep in the membrane of our psyche. But knowing the origin story of decisions that are out of our hands is a powerful position to hold. It provides opportunity for more strategy. If we are in denial about what's really going on or make assumptions about the core of a problem, then we never strategically tackle it. Instead, we fall into a type of childish rebellion. And that kind of rebellion can be unsafe.

After a meaningful discussion with the woman, my ultimate response was, "It is what it is." But I didn't mean we should retreat. I'm aware of all of the individual sensitivities that people bring to an experience, but the reality of circumstances dictates that we have to get past preconceived notions. We have to navigate the reality of the spaces we enter into. I realize this advice is hard when unseen powers are affecting your livelihood, harming your ability to earn an income and take care of yourself and your family. For many of us, when a situation appears to be threatening our very survival, we unconsciously go through a metamorphosis. And while the process is not as dramatic as the transformation of the *Lovecraft Country* character Ruby Baptiste, it feels like it is.

When we're uninterrupted, we don't let powerful men fighting about things far removed from our everyday lives affect our way of doing everything—from making a living to our way of being.

In the work that I do in Black Girl Ventures Foundation to help women find what I call *real money* to finance their endeavors, I have to keep asking the question: Are we proliferating a mold in business that subtly suggests that you have to be white? Or are we setting an example for the women we serve that you need to be free to do whatever you want?

Now, instead of being "funded like white people," I get funded like me. There are always invisible factors interrupting, in both positive and negative ways, our journey. Some of those invisible factors may become known to us, some never will. We have both received things and had things taken away without our knowledge, and this will continue to happen throughout our entrepreneurship journey. Your job is to not let these interruptions, both known and unknown, dictate your success.

One way to build your brand uninterrupted is to be you. As I mentioned at the top of this chapter, the success of my brand even has my closest friends forgetting the other aspects of me that they know intimately. The visibility of my brand supersedes, at times, even the one-to-one real-life relationships I have. As humans we are way better at seeing. Magicians fool us with our eyes, we believe what we think we are seeing. Anything outside of what we see is invisible, and that is the crux of building a successful brand using online tools. The brand needs to be authentic while showing the aspects we want to convey. You need to use this invisibility paradox while being uninterrupted to your advantage when it comes to building your brand.

Authenticity as a System Hack

When it comes to brand building, authenticity is key. Facebook, the global social network with nearly two billion users per day, wasn't originally designed to be the massive algorithm-advertising-based company that it is today. It was built to create a space for college students to connect online the way they did in person—targeted at people who were introverts, like one of its founders. Twitter was initially imagined to be an SMS-based communications platform, allowing for its founder and a group of friends to keep tabs on each other through their status updates. Both of these mega businesses were built from an emotional center that was intimately connected to something that their founders wanted but from which they were excluded.

If you want to convey your vision to the rest of us, you need to show up as you. To chart your own path is to realize that authenticity is the true disruptor.

I'm often asked how I show up to meetings with organizations like Experian and Visa completely as myself. I'm frequently asked, "How do you feel it's okay to wear your hair that way, to wear that bright-colored lipstick, to wear those clothes, to say whatever you're thinking?"

My answer is, "How could I not?"

Three principles guide me in those situations. The first one is to be a mirror for the person sitting in front of me. I know it sounds counterintuitive to being authentic, although I'm not saying that by mirroring my audience I am prioritizing their needs over mine, but rather that I am seeing both of our needs in the mirror. They also see both of our needs in the same mirror. Mirroring helps the people in front of you to see you, and you to see them. The image looks like something you are in agreement with. I learned this from performing poetry in front of crowds that don't look like me or that don't have the same experiences as me. Performing poems that can invoke a universal reaction involves highlighting common experiences that create neutral ground. When you can do this you (1) will get the reaction from the listener that you want and (2) you will provide the listener with something that they can hold onto, something they can relate to. In this way, I maintain my authenticity *and* tap into something genuine within my audience just by becoming a mirror in the moment—a skill that has been invaluable and transferable. I use that same mirroring principle when attending venture capital fund meetings. I look for ways to meet the other person's needs and to allow the other person to see themselves in my needs.

The mirroring strategy leads to my second principle, that doing business with authenticity requires deep relationship building.

In order to build meaningful connections, the first thing to do is to find commonalities. When I walk into spaces that feel unfamiliar, I ask, "What are the things that we have in common? How can I focus on those things to overcome our differences?"

I approach every meeting with the core belief that there is something here that we have in common, even if it is the most basic thing I can imagine. Like talking about the weather, for example. If we both agree on how hot it is, then we have a starting point. Next, the differences between us can be used as talking points to lean into what I want to walk away with. Then, in the discussion of our differences, I look for something we both can appreciate.

Those three elements—finding commonalities, leaning into differences, and finding shared appreciation—can help us move beyond the immediate reactions we have when we feel out of place entering into systemic structures that have been very good at excluding marginalized groups.

The third principle is to create something. One of the most effective ways to feel more confident and to move through the internal feelings of doubt or impostor syndrome and the external challenges of racist or sexist micro-aggressions is to engage in art. As an artist, I have permission to create something new or to be what some might even call outlandish. Once I create something, it's mine. I take ownership of it because it is an expression of my most authentic self. Without creating something, we never really feel like we have the permission to forge ahead. We can't see the space for us to insert ourselves.

Walking into a room as the "other" can feel like the risks are high. Therefore, hacking the system of historical patriarchy and the deeply embedded structure of white supremacy requires that we ask, "How do we challenge each other to know that there's a different person in the room?" We are compelled to be diplomatically radical—to show up in the room and say, "Yes, we're all in this together. And, yes, we're all going to operate from our own cultural lenses." Therefore, that means we all have to be mindful that there will be comments or questions that make us uncomfortable, but if those interactions move the conversation along toward diplomacy, then the risks are worth it. I'm not afraid to be in the room with anyone when I lean into being rooted in authenticity because I understand that my presence tells a new story. It not only tells my story, but it challenges the narrative of what these rooms *should* look like. My presence asks the questions *Why do these rooms always look the same? How can we tell a different story? What is the new story I'm telling the world?*

The way I show up to meetings with the largest companies in the world completely as myself is because I believe in the new narrative I am inserting into historically white, male spaces. White men have historically been the face of the hero. However, my presence says, "That's the old hero's journey." The old hero's journey enmeshed in white male heterosexuality says that heroes are rare and special: they rise above everyone else, using power and force to forge their path and prove that they are the chosen ones. And they are almost always white men, claiming the status of heroes and authoring the stories of heroes. The woman changemakers of the world stick to women's spaces and keep their dreams small and private—if they dream at all. However my existence tells a new story. A new kind of fairytale for women who want to change the world, one that proclaims that every woman has some special magic that she can manifest and catalyze to change not just her world, but the whole world. She just needs the faith, will, and determination that come when someone believes in her dream and her ability to do. She needs a fairy godmother, one who is loving, honest, clear-sighted, and fierce in her belief that her Cinderellas can make their dreams come true if they're willing to do the work. ENTER Omí Bell. That is how I remind myself to step into these spaces. Ask yourself, "What is the new story you want to tell? What does it mean to be authentically you?" This coupled with the tactics I've shared so far in this book will allow you to be authentic while building a powerful brand that generates revenue.

PART II

Motivate

CHAPTER 4

Your Power Is in Your Purpose

Black people always die first in horror films, and the same is true in the world of investor funding for Black and Brown entrepreneurs. If you've read this far, you've learned strategy around building fail-safe businesses, how to think beyond the surface of discrimination, how to be strategic in terms of branding as well as lots of other tactics to navigate the intricacies of building a successful business. However, none of these techniques matter if you do not have a purpose you are dedicated to along with a mindset that is suitable to carry you through this often lonely and difficult journey. The combination of staying true to my purpose and the power of my thinking are, at times, the only two things that have prevented me from either giving up or blowing up on, let's be frank, white people.

Lucky for you, I'm the Black character in the room full of white privilege, exclusivity, and power that doesn't die in this horror film. I'll be there surviving and thriving in the original, the sequel, and any other iteration of this proverbial horror film genre. In fact, the whole point of Black Girl Ventures is for people like me to multiply. That is the entire motivation for the constructs laid out in this book. To teach people like you how to make it into exclusive rooms that I have had the privilege of accessing while sustaining your kick-ass business. While the iconic phrase "We don't die, we multiply" by Robin Harris might be a funny nod to the Black comedy *Bebe's Kids* (I don't know if you caught it), it is extremely accurate in how I think about disrupting the investor funding model and access to capital for people like me. Being the only Black woman in a room full of the world's top CEOs and entrepreneurs often feels like I am the sole Black character in a horror movie, designed to see me perish. The proverbial threat is not Freddie Krueger or Jason but a spheroid of white silence, white privilege, and systemic discrimination at work, unfolding before my very eyes. Just when I think I've seen and heard it all, BOOM, Freddie Krueger has me trapped in a situation as I scramble to get out, not only alive but with my integrity.

Just like the horror film genre, the investor funding world needs disruptors. We need you to build powerful businesses and access to new places, people, and ideas in which you may often be the only one, but you survive and live to tell us about it. Your access is our survival guide, in the same way my access is your survival guide. Black people died in horror films for decades, ad nauseum, until Jordan Peele came along and disrupted the entire genre with the movie *Get Out*. When I watched *Get Out* I looked at it through the eyes of a Black woman entrepreneur who has to consistently avoid the "sunken place" while operating in a white environment. An environment that is a requirement if I want to continue to grow my brand and business at scale. While Chris, the main Black character in the film, ended up in the "sunken place" after willingly dating Rose, a white woman, and entering that plantation, I have no choice but to enter. Therefore, I have developed mechanisms that allow me to speak truth to power, when necessary, but I'd be lying if I said I wasn't scared or frustrated at times. I, too, have to be strategic while also being socially conscious of my privilege as someone who gets to rub shoulders with CEOs from around the world.

In the summer of 2022, I was at the Aspen Ideas Festival, a place where brilliant minds and changemakers gather once a year to exchange ideas. I got invited to a private dinner, in which I found myself sitting between the president of the Aspen Institute and the president of Sesame Workshop, the nonprofit educational organization behind Sesame Street. At this affair were others such as the chairwoman of MasterCard, the CEO of Allstate, the head of the Walmart Foundation, the chief strategy officer for Planned Parenthood, and more. This felt very much like the proverbial "table" that I had been working so hard to get to. While these moments can be intimidated, I felt strongly that if I had been invited I belonged. We were all talking about the Edelman Trust Barometer and social leadership as business owners. For brief context, the Edelman Trust Barometer is a survey that is conducted by the Edelman public relations company. The survey is conducted every year, and it measures the level of trust that people have in different institutions. The Edelman Trust Barometer has been around for more than 20 years, and it has also been used to measure how much people are willing to pay for products or services from a certain institution. It measures the level of trust in major institutions, such as government, business, media, non-governmental organizations (NGOs), and educational institutions. What came up in our discussion, among these businesspersons, is that the Edelman Trust Barometer has found that the public believes deeply that business has a role in social issues. Employees don't want to work for companies that are misaligned with their values and belief systems when it comes to societal issues. Basically, people believe that CEOs should have an opinion on societal issues, and they do not want to work for companies that don't care about what they care about. Jake, let's call him, was a researcher at Edelman and was going through some of the numbers from these surveys on the topic of social leadership when he then opened up the topic to the attendees at the dinner.

Together we started getting deeper and deeper into the topic of trust, and I was sitting there listening and processing before raising my hand to chime in. I said, "You know, because I am maybe one of three Black women at a table of 40 people, when I hear this conversation about trust, I'm sitting here, and I really want to bring the perspective that people like me are not automatically trusted and those that have spoken so far are speaking from a level of some trust to more trust, but I'm walking into rooms where there's no trust for me at all." I continued after a brief pause, "I have to prove that I'm supposed to be trusted because I am a Black woman." Everyone seemed shocked at this new information they were receiving, yet never considered. The room went silent as if you could hear a pin drop. I explained that in my world, it's like playing a game. Those who are given trust because they simply exist are playing baseball, but I'm playing basketball. Do I know all the rules of baseball? No. Can I go enjoy the game? Yes. Do you know all the rules of basketball? Maybe not. Can you enjoy a basketball game? Yes. But we're playing two totally different games. I can't win *your* game without knowing all of the rules—I can come close. Occasionally, I might score a few points or win an inning, but I don't know enough about the game to actually win the game. Actually, when I win an inning, the rules of the game change. "We're in two totally different arenas. I'm not automatically trusted when I walk into the room," I finished. The eyes in the room spoke volumes amidst the deafening silence. Clearly, they had the privilege of never even having to consider this reality.

The moderator of the discussion, a Black woman, broke the silence by gently thanking me for my comments and responding with, "It's something that we should be thinking about." Though she is a moderator in this situation, she is also a character in the "horror film" with me, juggling empathetic moderation with tough conversations. She is also the kind of character that won't "die" in this film. In fact, in that moment I was learning to navigate from her. Being in rooms where you are one of the only people who look like you is less about blowing up conversations with jabs and more like an underground railroad where navigators are strategically placed. I also want to note that the reference to the horror film is NOT indicative of how I was treated. It's more about the ability to continue to exist in this room where it's obvious that you're different and you want to authentically share your expert thought while not knowing whether you will be accepted as a thought leader. Everyone at the table was very kind and open to dialogue.

Throughout the evening more conversation took place. I was listening and absorbing, trying to take in as much of the moment as possible when the proverbial horror film moved to the climax. The CEO of a major insurance company spoke on the topic of social leadership. We'll call him HT. HT begins talking about how he doesn't feel like business should have a role in social issues. He said that no one should be expecting Coca-Cola to solve voting rights, and as the words slipped off the tip of his tongue I immediately looked around the table. You know, how you're out with your homegirls and someone says or does something reckless and you make eye contact indicating that you too heard the BS. Only in this room, the tribe of Black woman CEOs isn't there. I scanned the room, looking for "my tribe," finally making eye-contact with the chief strategy officer for Planned Parenthood. At least I knew I had an ally that felt what I was feeling at the moment. I'm thinking, "What is this dude talking about right now? Is he freaking serious?" I feel angst and anxiety building up. I know I have to say something. I could not sit here and not say anything. After all, when we are in rooms like this, we feel a responsibility to represent and speak truth to power, whether we want to or not. By default, this becomes a part of our labor whether we asked for that job or not. I'm in a room of all these high-net-worth, high positioned CEOs of major products and things I use every day. These are the thoughts going through my head as I do a quick cost-benefit analysis of what my next move should be. I know one thing: I do not have the privilege of sitting in silence at this moment. I just don't. I assessed the room analyzing who would have my back when I spoke out against this man's comments. I was confident the moderator would have my back by at least bringing the conversation back to its center after I spoke. It's important to have recognizable allies in rooms like this. I knew the senior vice president (SVP) at PayPal would have my back as he is the one who invited me to the dinner. Let me be clear, having your back in this kind of room does not mean I expected any of these people to piggyback or endorse what I was about to say. I just mean, having my back in terms of empathy and a possible side conversation supporting me in private. It's important to note that historically Black people have needed both kinds of support. We have needed people to be openly vocal and people to help us in private. In moments like this trust is either built or damaged. Identifying who does trust you vs. who doesn't becomes a shield around your emotions as you navigate high-powered rooms like these. I was grateful to be trusted by the SVP to bring my whole self to the table.

In these situations my thinking becomes important to the context as well. I reminded myself that my contribution was going to be important, and that's why someone felt it was important to invite me there in the first place. The burden of being invited somewhere so that the Black perspective is shared can be daunting, and it is something I still have not gotten used to after over a decade of doing this work and being in these rooms. The power of my thinking, however, didn't allow me to feel afraid to speak. Being silent does not make you less afraid. This CEO continued on, "Well, you know, businesses and CEOs should just stay in their lane, and their lane is not social issues." I'm so hot at this point. I spoke. "I think you're conflating a couple things. I don't think that people believe that Coca-Cola can fix voting rights. I believe the word 'fix' is where we get misaligned with what employees are wanting or what the public is wanting Coca-Cola to do. Businesses have multiple people that work for them and that live in the geographical area they are serving. They do have a duty to care about their employees, therefore caring about voting rights. It's interesting because CEOs want us to stay in our place, yet they are all over the place. Jeff Bezos goes to space and wants the world to watch and cheer him on when he's supposed to be running a logistics company. How is that staying in your lane? What lane are you in? There ain't no lane." HT finally gave some sort of flippant response and went on enjoying his beverages and dessert utensils for the evening.

After the dinner there was a mingling session, and the daughter of a well-known women's rights advocate came up to me and thanked me for speaking up and then added, "I sat in white silence while you spoke. And I didn't say anything and I agreed." She said she didn't really know what to say and that she wanted to thank me for sharing.

The ambivalence inside me was resounding. Her comments made me feel a little good, but at the same time her comments made me feel sad. I am out here on an island all by myself, but people telling me in my ear they agree with me is somewhat validating. When you need somebody to speak up in support, you are out there by yourself. So many people came up to me, thanking me in my ear. Thanking me for my courage. They kept saying the word "courage."

When I got back to my room, I had a moment because I sat with things, and the word "courage" kept playing in my head. I could hear the myriad people thanking me and calling me courageous repeatedly like a broken record player. I had been severely underestimating the amount of courage displayed in my comments, but having a moment of clarity, I remembered I mentioned Jeff Bezos, and somebody in that room could have been his friend. Somebody in that room might have been texting him as I spoke his name out my mouth.

Then rapid thoughts went through my brain as I lay on the bedside of the hotel room, *Oh my God, what did I do? Did I cut myself off from other funding? Did I say something that was too uncomfortable for them? Did I say something that offended somebody? Was it diplomatic enough?* I had to really unpack the situations as well as my thoughts and feelings. I meditated and journaled to filter through the feelings I was having. Something told me to turn on the television. I turned on BET, and the BET awards were on. I thought to myself, *Damn, that looks so fun.* The camera turned and was angled on one of my friends who was at the awards show that night, and I was thinking, *Man, I could've been there instead of in a room full of people that I felt I had to educate.* I had made a conscious decision to be at the Aspen Ideas Festival dinner instead of the BET awards. I chose to be where I was. As this mix of emotions swirled around my head, I began to cry because in that moment I had wished that I could be at the BET awards with all these Black people, a part of my culture and with my friends, celebrating that, not where I was. Trying to survive the preverbal horror show again, feeling like I could go either way—I could shrivel up and be the Black person that breaks or I could be Jordan Peele's version of the horror movie. In moments like this my purpose statement centers me. After journaling and meditating to decompress, I went back to my life's purpose. Which is as follows:

> *To create spaces of belonging and self-actualization.*
>
> *To exhibit community as the key to changing the world.*
>
> *To breed confidence that births new leaders/leadership.*
>
> *To catalyze generations of unstoppable BIPOC people in business.*

The beauty of a purpose statement that drives your life's vision and aligns with the power of your thinking is that when you find yourself in a room alone, it is the combination of those two things that reminds you why you have worked so hard to be placed in the position you find yourself. Why you have worked so hard to even be invited to rooms like that. And why you must survive within and outside of these environments. *Would I have rather been at the very exclusive Aspen Ideas Festival dinner where not everybody like me gets to go?* I must stay committed and true to my life's vision and purpose. My life's purpose reminds me to continue pushing forward and having these conversations in places like that. My life's vision reminds me to make change, even when it's scary or difficult. People like me need to be in those kinds of rooms so that the people at those BET awards can continue to get the corporate funding. That is the intersection of where my purpose meets my thinking. Sometimes it is not what I want to do, it is what I need to do to live up to the purpose that I have committed to. Upon this clarity and recentering, my perception of the BET awards show on television changed. This is a great transition into the importance of your thinking and how powerful it is on your entrepreneurship journey. The power of my thinking helped shape what happened next with HT.

To be a successful Black woman business owner is to question and at the same time to poke at and experiment with preconceived notions imposed on you by people, systems, ideas, and even history. This type of confidence is the only way to chart your own path in the venture capital world. You need to burst onto the scene with a mindset like the latest rapper who is charging onto the world's stage boasting about his achievements, possessions, or abilities with excessive pride and self-satisfied talk, even though he may not have two pennies to rub together. Before I go into how to better develop your thinking and the power within it, I want to dig deeper into experimenting with preconceived notions about events and especially people. Sometimes our preconceived notions of people (e.g. my perception of HT after his comments) coupled with our anger at someone's remarks can cloud our judgment, thus preventing us from making powerful allies or at minimum, connections. After processing all that happened at the Aspen Ideas Festival dinner, I had another encounter with HT. But it wasn't what you might expect. At this point in my career, I have evolved from Shelly to Omi, understanding that decisions, reactions, and notions cannot be a result of fear or anger, but instead I need to be strategic and in integrity with my purpose. Shelly would have been too angry to ever think about communicating with HT on a one-to-one level, but Omi was mature, focused, and dedicated to the vision.

The next day at the Aspens Ideas Festival there was a panel, an actual panel, on trust, the topic at the dinner from the evening before. I decided to attend. Some of the people from my dinner table were on the panel, in addition to HT and the researcher from the Edelman Trust Barometer. The researchers from Edelman gave me a signal to ask the panel a question. I got the feeling that he wanted me to bring up the comments I had made the day before, to jump back into the topic of social leadership and the role of business. I didn't know this then, but looking back he wanted to bring that same topic up again because he wanted to urge HT to address the theme again. To my surprise HT didn't have the same comments as he had the night before. He shifted and added more context to his thought process. HT said that he still doesn't feel like business should have a role in certain social issues, but he elaborated and said that to his employees the stance of the business does matter. He went on to talk about *Roe v Wade* being overturned and said that his company made a statement on the issue and that his company would give people stipends to travel for abortions, if needed. I said to HT at the panel that that was a change from yesterday's comments, as the example he gave was actually one of his businesses engaging in social responsibility. I told him that as the CEO, that was him deciding that his business has a role in social issues. I reminded him that that was a good thing that he did for his employees. After the panel, I decided that I wanted to look this dude in the eyes and have a conversation. This is a pivotal mindset shift. As I had let go of any anger, I was willing to come to that panel to hear HT and others speak again. I decided that I really wanted to give him some feedback. I went over, waited in line to talk to him after the panel, and I told him that I think he's just been doing this corporate thing so long and that he has seen so much that his answers are just more blunt but that he does care about the business role on social issues. At this point, I was coming from a place of connection and commonality as we discussed in Chapter 2. There was no judgment in me thinking. He asked me to walk and talk with him. We took a 30-minute walk where we had a great exchange. He gave me feedback, and I gave him feedback. There was a mutual respect. I wouldn't have been able to approach him if I had been angry. I wouldn't have been able to approach him if I was out of alignment with my purpose and if I did not have the ability to think through the situation. You cannot let fear or anger guide your next step in the game of entrepreneurship, or even life. You might be thinking, "How do I get to a place where my mindset can be guided by my vision and purpose, as opposed to negative factors such as anger, inferiority or whatever other negative feeling creeps up into the mind?" The answer is that your power is in your thinking, which we will delve into next.

Your Power Is in Your Thinking

Early in my career I started working with an intuition coach to understand how to use my intuition in business. She told me, "You keep thinking that your power is in your doing, but your power is in your thinking." She gave me an exercise to do. "Tell me some of the things that you think about yourself," she said. At that time, I thought, "People don't want to see me successful," and other similar types of judgments that people say to themselves constantly. It's especially difficult when you're a person of color—who has faced the trauma and micro-aggressions of racism—to resist falling into a mindset where you believe that people don't want to see you win, when in reality it's primarily what we think about ourselves. I'm not saying that racism isn't real or that we haven't faced micro-aggressions. What I am saying is that antagonistic behaviors can trigger systemic trauma and seduce us into living inside preconceived ideas about what other people are thinking about us. It's imperative that we not get stuck in those traumas.

Another exercise my coach gave me was to repeat this affirmation three times: "I am valuable." She instructed me to write the first statement at the top of my journal and then write whatever came to mind. Repeat the first statement, and again write whatever came to mind, and to do that 20 or 30 times, until I reached a point where the only thing that came to mind was agreement. Then move on to the next two statements and repeat the process.

The first time I did the exercise I wrote, "I am valuable," and the first thing that came to mind was, "This is stupid. I don't want to be writing this."

Then again: "I am valuable." And I wrote: "Okay, this lady's saying this is going to work. I don't know this lady like that." I started questioning her.

Third time: "I am valuable." Then I wrote: "I don't know if I am valuable. Valuable at what? What is valuable? What does that mean?"

I did this exercise more than 20 times a day, every day for a period of time. I finally reached a place where I had nothing else to say but "I am."

And that's how I began to change my mindset. I have kept that exercise with me throughout my career. Any time I start feeling sensations of negativity coming up, I pause, come up with three affirmations around what I'm feeling, and then filter out the noise. If you can quiet the outside noise of other people's fears and inhibitions, then you can find a process that works for you.

When I first launched BGV, I announced the event on Meetup .com. Thirty women came. I ran the whole thing like a poetry slam. Women who wanted to pitch their business idea signed up for three minutes to do so. Audience members voted for the pitch that was the most persuasive by giving money. We took a percentage to cover costs and gave the rest to the founder.

We've covered much of my journey from the inception of BGV in previous chapters, but what I didn't mention was that three years after that first humiliating venture capital meeting (discussed in Chapter 1), I raised half a million dollars from the Ewing Marion Kauffman Foundation (Kauffman Foundation). From that journey, three lessons came into sharp focus. The first one is that it took me three years to get that level of funding only because it took me two years to realize that when people in philanthropy ask, "How can I be helpful?" what they really mean is, "How much do you want?" Understanding how your industry communicates is critical.

The second lesson is that even after achieving that level of funding, I still struggled with moments where I questioned whether I should have a seat at the table. A recent engagement with Nike is one of those examples. I was on a panel with WNBA players—real-life champions. Not champions like your best friend saying, "Oh, you're a champion," but literally people who have won championship rings. Also, they all knew one another, so when one of them responded to the moderator's questions, the others supported her with compliments. When a question was directed to me, I thought, "What could I possibly add to this conversation? I'm not a physical athlete in the way that the WNBA would consider." So I wondered, "Why am I here?" Then I wondered, "Are they thinking, 'Why is she here?'" The infamous impostor phenomenon kicked in, tugging at my confidence and daring me to trust myself.

But in moments like those it's just as easy to see yourself as a trailblazer. People always say, "If you're the smartest person in your circle, you need a new circle." Nobody teaches you how to be the dumbest person in the circle.

When trailblazing—or pioneering your own path—it is highly possible that you will be the dumbest person in your circle…at first. To pioneer means there is a forest in front of you, nobody has forged through that forest in the way you're doing it, and no one knows who you are or what you can do. In that case, of course they may not understand why you're in their arena. Trailblazing means sometimes you must be quiet, to listen and learn until you find commonalities. When you find ideas or experiences that you have in common, you will have a way into the conversation. Once you're in the conversation, it will be obvious that you're supposed to be there.

The third lesson is that if I let rebellion drive my decisions, I am not being strategic. When I started BGV, I launched it with the idea that I didn't need anybody. I could run my slam-poetry-rent-party like meet-ups all day long. It was a form of protest against those who said I couldn't do it.

But I began to realize that if my team at BGV and I were going to grow our efforts, we needed more money. If we were going to give serious money to people, we needed a strategy. The Kauffman Foundation grant created the space for us to experiment with a strategic approach to funding Black and Brown women entrepreneurs. The fund vastly opened our ability to move into and anchor our work in cities across the United States.

The Kauffman Foundation allowed me to scale my programming. And because of their mission *"to help individuals attain economic independence by advancing educational achievement and entrepreneurial success, consistent with the aspirations of its founder Ewing Marion Kauffman,"* it was a perfect partnership. And I desperately needed a like-minded partner, one who was constantly moving the needle, asking the questions no one else was asking, always going where no one had ever gone before. I needed that.

As a result, I have gone from that first fundraising meeting with the Fortune 500 venture capitalist dude berating me for even seeking an investment, to only three years later having major funding partners like the NBA Foundation, Google, and community foundations seek me out. And every partner that has come to me since that time has said, "We see what you're doing. We love what you're doing, but we really want to know what your ideas are."

In 2021, on a call with one of our donors, the representative said, "I wanted to set a meeting with you because we're about to launch a program, and I just want to know what you think."

I was thinking, "What? Lady, I'm trying to run an organization with a lot of moving parts across the nation, and you just want to know what I think? I mean, you're not interested in what I've done or what I need?"

Of course, I told her what I thought because I'm always coming up with some interesting ways to think about how to approach a new program.

By the end of that call, it suddenly occurred to me, *Oh, this is valuable.* And I was reminded of what my intuition coach had said, "You keep thinking it's about what you do. It's not what you do. It's about how you think about what you do, and how you think about executing. That's the real sweet spot for you."

And guess what, reader, it's the sweet spot for you too. You might go through some things, but you will come out alive and your tribe will be there for you sometimes. Yet other times, you will be in a room alone with your thoughts after speaking truth to power or challenging the status quo, and when that happens, you need to fall back on the power of your purpose and thinking.

The combination of your purpose and thinking will get you through the tough days, the tough nights, the tough situations as you forge your path ahead to mega-success as an entrepreneur. Remember, "We don't die, we multiply" and "the Black guy doesn't die in this movie."

CHAPTER 5

Nothing Moves Without People

I don't do the word "can't," and you shouldn't either. In a defining moment from the film *The Pursuit of Happyness*, Chris Gardner, played by Will Smith, explains to his son how important it is not to let anyone or anything get in the way of his dreams. I was told I couldn't finish college as a teenage mom. I was told that no one would rent a tee-pee as an Airbnb. I was told I couldn't raise three kids as a single mom and follow my dreams. I was told I couldn't run a successful business focused on women of color. I was told I couldn't get access to capital. I was told I couldn't do whatever it is I was trying to do so many times I have lost count. If I had listened, I wouldn't be here right now writing this book. I wouldn't be running one of my most successful Black-owned businesses in the country focusing on a segment of the population that has historically been ignored. I wouldn't be doing any of this if I believed what others told me—I can't. That's not all though. You also shouldn't tell yourself you can't. The truth is YOU CAN. You can do whatever you want, in whatever way you want, and how you want if you have a plan.

When I changed my name to Omilâdè I was already verified on Instagram as Shelly Bell, and as you may know, once you are verified you can't change your name on these social media apps. I tried and tried to get it changed while keeping my verification symbol. I went through all the verification steps time and time again. I even went to a Facebook concierge. They all told me the same thing, "They already verified your ID, so **you can't** change your name." **You can't**, and any variation of the phrase means absolutely nothing to me. It's like telling me that a restaurant only has what's listed on the menu. We all know that isn't true. If you didn't, you know now. Months later I was at the Aspen Ideas Festival walking around with a business associate. We stopped in front of a great place to take a picture.

It was a big life-sized cut-out that read IDEAS. We wanted a picture in front of the sign, so we asked a woman standing nearby to help us out. While she was taking our pictures I immediately noticed that she was purposeful in how she was shooting us. She moved around to different angles and asked us to pose in different positions. She was adjusting the lighting on my cell phone and doing *all the things*. This jumped out to me because I recognize above average everywhere I go. I said, "Oh, okay. Angles!" in a jokingly light manner, acknowledging that she had turned our simple photo request into a full-blown photoshoot. I then asked her where she worked. It was a genuine question. She told me that she worked for Instagram. I said, "Ohhh, I've been having this challenge with IG." I went on to tell her that while she may not be able to do anything about it, I thought I'd run it by her to get her advice. After all, *she's an insider*, I thought to myself. She was open to hearing what I had to say. I told her the whole story about how I changed my name in real life and that I was a public figure, but that Instagram wouldn't let me make the change to my profile while keeping my verification status. She listened, thought for a moment, and then told me that she could put in a ticket on my behalf. I thanked her, and we exchanged information so that I could follow up, which I did.

After the festival I contacted her, and she put in a ticket. At first, they responded saying that Omi Bell was not even an available name on Instagram. I thought this was strange because I knew it was available (Read: **you can't**). I could see on the platform that the name Omi Bell wasn't taken. However, at least I was making a little bit of progress, and someone on the inside was looking into the issue. In the meantime, I was brainstorming other names like Omilade Bell or Shelly Omi Bell and so on. I was going to settle for a variation of the name I really didn't want, but instead I asked my connect to try to get IG to cooperate again. My connect appealed their decision and put a ticket back in. *Voila,* they changed it. You can find me at Omi Bell on Instagram if you feel so inclined. I kept my verification status, and my name was updated to Omi Bell just as I had hoped. Not only is the rejection of "you can't" important, but you also need to understand that nothing moves without people.

Drake is a master at creating catchy punchlines and having all of us singing bad-advice-heavy lyrics at the top of our lungs with conviction. I've been there, from the depths of my soul rapping things like, "Started from the bottom now I'm here" or "No new friends." For a moment back in 2013, Drake had folks really believing that he made it on his own and that growing his social capital didn't matter. It seemed to make people feel good that someone like Drake gave them permission to stay surrounded by average friends, doing average things. Hence, no new friends. The reality is that your network is your net worth, and you need to implement a strategy to increase your social capital so that you can grow as a business and individual. Most people do average things and live average lives. And to quote Seth Godin, *"Is there a difference between 'average' and 'mediocre'? Not so much."* The truth is, not everyone who has the ability is willing to help you. Some people want to help you, but they don't have the ability. The woman I met at Instagram had the ability to help and was willing. Nothing moves without people.

If Harriet Tubman took Drake's advice of "no new friends," she would have never been able to utilize the Underground Railroad to help hundreds of enslaved Africans escape. There was a network of cells used to operate the Underground Railroad. Isaac Hopper, a convert to Quakerism, established what one author called "the first operating cell of the abolitionist underground." Others such as John Brown, Thomas Garrett, and the list goes on and on all participated in the network that led the enslaved to freedom. Even Harriet Tubman needed a network of connected people who had the ability and interest in helping her, regardless of color. Harriett Tubman connected with people to serve her mission based on ideology, not color.

Building your social capital is not just about being invited into rooms with high-profile people, it's also about connecting with people on a human level. You need to be able to identify above-average people, perceive opportunities, and work with people who have access to things that you do not have access to. Nick Cannon, mega-successful television host, rapper, actor, and comedian, attributes a large part of his success to his relationship with Will Smith. In Nick Cannon's own words, "I wouldn't be where I am today if it wasn't for that guy. His hands-on approach and being a big brother and a friend early on in my career were everything. He gave me my first record deal; he gave me my first television deal..." Will Smith gave Nick Cannon a record deal when he was 16 years old. At this time, in the 90s, Will Smith was the biggest box-office actor in the country. Will Smith saw Nick Cannon at a comedy festival and instantly knew Nick Cannon was special—above average. Will Smith had the ability to perceive someone who was above average, someone who was extraordinary. You need to develop this same ability as you move through the world. A part of this is letting go of people in your business who have roles that require above-average talent but who are doing average or below-average work. Not everyone you employ needs to be above average, but there are certain roles where the job requires someone special. You might be wondering, *How do you identify above average talent?* and *How do you connect with people who are behind the door you are trying to open?* These are great questions, and part of the answer is in what I call L.I.A.—linkage, ability, and interest. This is a common formula used in philanthropy. I discovered that this formula was not only great for fundraising but great for community building and growing your network.

You can't activate L.I.A. until you understand the importance of perceiving opportunities and making a genuine human connection. In a famous letter that is widely available online, Thomas Garrett describes how Harriet Tubman became known to him and how she helped slaves escape using a network of underground connections. Thomas Garrett was a resident of Quaker Hill in Wilmington, Delaware, which was the dividing line between the North and the South. Garrett aided runaway slaves and made a name for himself as the "station master" of the eastern route of the Underground Railroad, for which he worked for 40 years. Garrett says, *"The date of the commencement of her labors, I cannot certainly give; but I think it must have been about 1845; from that time till 1860, I think she must have brought from the neighborhood where she had been held as a slave, from 60 to 80 persons, from Maryland, some 80 miles from here. No slave who placed himself under her care, was ever arrested that I have heard of; she mostly had her regular stopping places on her route; but in one instance, when she had two stout men with her, some 30 miles below here, she said that God told her to stop, which she did; and then asked him what she must do."* Harriett Tubman was a successful conductor on the Underground Railroad and a symbol of heroism that required relationships with other people. She needed to rely on white abolitionists to move slaves from Maryland to Philadelphia to Canada. The Underground Railroad is all about leveraging social capital. Without linking with other people who had the interest and ability to help her reach her goals Tubman would not have been successful. This is true for you as well. Start making and leveraging connections based on your goals and mission right now.

Perceived Opportunities

After talking about linkage, ability, and interest (what we will call L.I.A. from here on) at a recent speaking engagement a small business owner asked me, "Do you ever value a completely cold call to an investor in your space?" My response was that I've had people who I ended up working with through LinkedIn who certainly were unknown to me. They just kept reaching out until I said to myself, "Let me just talk to this person because they aren't giving up." Investors do take note of that, and I would never tell you not to just shoot your shot. However, I believe in strategy and implementing strategy so that you can assess results and reach big goals *on purpose*. Make sure you are intentional and concise in whatever you do. If you engage in cold-calling, make sure you have a system to activate that in a successful way *on purpose*. Regardless of the strategy you use, you need to show the person on the other end that there is value in your proposition for both parties—not just you. You must create interest for the other party.

Chris Gardner is an American entrepreneur and author. You may have never heard of him, but you probably know his story. He is best known for his book *The Pursuit of Happyness*, which was later adapted into the film starring Will Smith as referenced at the top of this chapter. Chris Gardner was born in 1949 in Louisiana. His father abandoned the family when he was just a child, and his mother died when he was 10 years old. Chris had to take care of himself and his younger brother from then on. He dropped out of school at the age of 15 to work full time as a janitor at the San Francisco airport, but he never gave up on his dream to become successful one day. Chris eventually became a stockbroker and made enough money to provide for himself and his son, Christopher Jr. However, not depicted in the film is that Chris went on to start his own firm and became a multimillionaire on Wall Street. Here's the amazing thing about Chris Gardner's real-life story: after landing the job as a stockbroker at Bear Stearns, he decided to start his own firm. He wanted to work for himself. He had a vision and perceived an opportunity. Today as an international motivational speaker he tells a story about how Bear Stearns became a public company, and it was at that time he started to see some opportunities that no one else perceived. As a stockbroker Chris Gardner saw some assets that no one believed were profitable. Chris's boss and colleagues called him crazy to leave Bear Stearns to create his own firm when no Black guys were doing this on Wall Street. Bear Stearns later collapsed during the 2008 financial crisis. During this time Chris was CEO of Christopher Gardner International Holdings, a financial services and brokerage company with offices in New York, Chicago, and San Francisco. When asked how his firm was successful in an interview with CBS New York, Gardner credits the opportunities he saw that no one else could see as well as the relationships he built along the way. You can think about cold-calling the way you think about Chris Gardner's life story. In the film Chris was persistent in getting into the stockbroker trainee program, and eventually he was accepted, despite trials and tribulations. However, as you can see from the real-life story of Chris Gardner, once working on Wall Street and then establishing his own firm, it was the quality of his relationships and the ability to perceive opportunities that took his life vision to the next level. Had Chris not perceived that there was an opportunity outside of Bear Stearns that required him to tap into a segment that was untouched, his life might have been completely different. He would have lost everything as an employee of a firm that tanked. I can't say that I always think cold-calling is bad because diligence can land you an opportunity. However, in terms of creating a vision for your business and activating your social capital, implementing a strategy around leveraging relationships is vital. As you move through life you must keep your goals top of mind so that you can perceive opportunities. Making connections and building relationships is about establishing a common connection (ideology, belief system, goal, vision, mission, etc.) and building a business partnership around ability and interest.

L.I.A.: Building Relationships

Building a relationship and a connection are two different things. You need to find that link and interest when you are looking at investors, when you are writing out your list of people who can help facilitate your business goals, and when you are activating your business plans in general. You need to implement the linkage, interest, and ability strategy I've coined L.I.A. Ask yourself, *Who are you linked to? Who shares your interests? How do you know this is the right investor? How do you know this is the right mentor? How do you know that this is the right advisor?* One of the ways to answer these very important questions is to figure out commonalities in terms of people you each know as well as understanding a person's business goals. Research shows that most of the time, especially on LinkedIn, people are looking at who you're already connected to before they accept your LinkedIn connection request. That means sometimes it's better for you to stop and look at who someone is linked to before you even make a connection request. If you want to work with a specific person, reaching out to them before you are connected with someone in their ecosystem might be premature. You haven't yet established a linkage point. People ask me all the time on LinkedIn if I know a specific person because I am linked to them on the platform. They want to try to establish a point of reference with me. They may be unfamiliar with me, but since we know the same people, it gets them familiarity and context. You can think about linkage as the thing that gets your foot in the door. The link could be geographical, family relationships, alma maters, etc. This link becomes important in your first introduction. You want to leverage that link.

When I met with one of the partners at Sequoia for the first time someone made the introduction. Sequoia is a private technology company that specializes in seed-stage, early-stage, and growth-stage investments. When someone connects you with a potential amazing partnership, it doesn't mean the person on the other end wants to work with you. This is where some people get tripped up. You must establish a relationship with that person. You have the connection, but you haven't engaged in relationship building. For this introduction, I took a step back and was intentional about how to build this relationship from the jump. I went through his LinkedIn and Twitter feeds to learn more about him beyond the surface level. I saw that his family liked show tunes. My son is a theater kid who loves show tunes. I don't, but that doesn't matter, it's a point of commonality that can be used to build a conversation. I started my email response to this warm connection saying something like, "Oh, wow, you know I have a son who loves show tunes, but I love hip hop. So, to say the least our Saturday mornings are fun." And then I went in with my introduction of who I am and what I wanted to talk about instead of leading with, "I'm Shelly Bell, the Founder of BGV. You should talk to me because I'm so great. Right?"

You also need to get clarity on whether this person is even interested in whatever you're interested in. Just because a third-party thing suggests that two people should meet, it doesn't necessarily mean they have something to professionally collaborate on. In terms of investors the questions would be, *Do you have overlapping business interests, and do they even have the ability to fund your organization?* This is where interest and ability become key. Previously I shared the steps in securing a relationship and funding from Nike. If you go back to that chapter, you can see this strategy in practice. We had similar interest in reaching a target audience, and Nike had the ability to fund Black Girl Ventures. L.I.A. is a quick and easy way to think through the early stages of relationship building with potential funders as well as those that can support your goals. At times, there may be linkage but no ability. There may be linkage and ability but no interest. That's okay. You can revisit that partnership down the line when it makes more sense for you and the potential partner. L.I.A. is the sweet spot. It's like getting dealt the best hand at the table in a game of spades. You know you have the best hand to win; you just need to play your cards right.

Building the Sweet Spot

As already discussed, a real opportunity to form a connection with someone who can help you in your journey will have three qualities: linkage, interest, and ability. *How do YOU build this intersection for yourself? How do you create this sweet spot?* As we go through L.I.A in a tactile sense in this section, you want to think about the way you can utilize this strategy right now with the people you've been putting off because you haven't figured out the best approach to connecting with them. Linkage asks, *Are you connected to this person?* Interest asks, *Is this person interested in what you are working on?* and ability asks, *Does this person have the ability to help or fund you?* Let's take a closer look at these one by one.

Linkage: An ideal opportunity to form a relationship can surface easily when you lead with a spirit of discovery. Finding a link between you and the person you would like to work with can jump-start your connection. Think broadly about potential connections. *Are they a family member? Do you share a mutual friend? Do you live in the same city? Did you attend the same school? Do you share a professional history? Do you share hobbies?* Anything that allows you to establish a deeper connection with the person than simply introducing yourself. Differentiate yourself from others. For example, famed TV personality and home living expert Martha Stewart met businesswoman Sharon Patrick while climbing Mount Kilimanjaro. Sharon went on to help Martha found the company Martha Stewart Living Omnimedia, where she worked as chief operating officer until 2004. Consider all the businesswomen and businessmen who missed out on this opportunity simply because they were not avid travelers and climbers like Martha Stewart herself.

Janice Bryant Howroyd, the first Black woman to run and own a billion-dollar company, got her professional start as a secretary for her brother-in-law Tom Noonan at *Billboard* magazine. When she used the business knowledge she acquired here to found her own company, The ActOne Group, Noonan became her first client. The familial connection and shared professional history were key in establishing Howroyd's and Noonan's professional relationship. When looking to form a business relationship with someone, find your common ground and don't be afraid to lead with it when approaching them.

Interest: You started your business because you see a need or a problem you are passionate about addressing or solving. The most organic connections will be with people who are interested in finding solutions to the same problems that you are already working on. Avoid an uphill battle by searching for people with the same professional interests as you. Alex Blumberg, founder and CEO of podcast network Gimlet Media, documented the journey of launching and growing the company on the podcast *StartUp*. While looking for a business partner to work on this endeavor with, he recounts meeting Matt Lieber. Matt, a former radio producer now working in business, is immediately intrigued and says he'd "been thinking someone should do this for a long time," as Blumberg puts it. Lieber goes on to become Blumberg's partner in the venture and the president of Gimlet Media. While credentials and qualifications are important, there is no substitute for shared passion. Where possible, find people who are interested in your field of work even before you meet them.

Ability: Perhaps the most straightforward idea to grasp in this trifecta is ability. The biggest opportunities will be with people who are actually in a position to help you. If your immediate concern is funding, those with enough money to fund your venture are most obviously poised to help you. However, as we will discuss further, ability can come in many forms. Even people who don't have the capital to fund your business can help you make connections with those who do, help you with feedback and advice, or bring knowledge to the table that you don't have. Make sure to evaluate the opportunities before you wholistically.

The ideal opportunity for a constructive relationship will hit the linkage-interest-ability trifecta. But what about relationships where you have two out of three? For example, someone may be interested in the same issues as you and have the ability to help, but you may not have any link to them. Is this relationship worth pursuing? First and foremost, this should be seen as an opportunity to find a link with this person. Do some research into their past, their present, their passions, their predicaments, and see if there is anything you can find to connect with them as I did with Sequoia. I recognize that many people may not have introductions made by others in order to engage with warm leads, and that is why we will talk further about social capital. But if you exhaust everything and don't find any inroads, you will have to weigh where you are in your business's journey and what other opportunities you have available to you. If there are more promising avenues to pursue, prioritize those; if there aren't, consider the potential upside and downside, and consider which factors are most useful to you where you are right now. Being thoughtful about the people and organizations you involve in your journey will make sure you are spending your energy where it can be most effective.

When you think about building relationships and building a business and how those things work together, you have to honestly assess the stage your business is in. You have to determine who you need to know based on that stage. Different stages of your business require that you know different people. Before your business goals and aspirations can even take shape you need to shift your mindset to know that it's all about people first. You need to have a genuine appreciation for the people you meet and be grateful for the opportunity to connect with others. It's true that you never know who you are talking to. I have been in plenty of spaces where up-and-coming early-stage entrepreneurs look past people. They are so busy headed to the panel where the celebrity is speaking, trying to get to the front of the line to get a chat with the famous person or the multimillionaire businessperson. Looking so much for a connect with the shiny object that you look past the strangers that are sitting right next to you is a huge mistake. Don't be so focused on the shiny object that you miss the gem right in front of you. I didn't need to connect with the CEO of Instagram to get my name changed on the platform.

Your end goal as a business owner is to make money. You aren't running a successful business if it isn't making money at some point; however, you need above-average people and systems in key roles to make money. You need to innately perceive opportunities and above-average output. Which is why the next chapter is called "Resist Average Relationships." You need to resist average relationships with others as well as yourself. You need to build your network, understand who is a part of your network and how to activate your network. We'll dig deeper into social capital so that you can be extraordinary and activate that social capital in order to create business partnerships that matter. Remember, as Will Smith's character said in the film *Pursuit of Happyness*, "Don't ever let somebody tell you, you can't do something… You got a dream? You gotta protect it. People can't do something themselves; they want to tell you, you can't do it. You want something? Go get it! Period!"

CHAPTER 6

Resist Being Average: Play Your Cards Right

A great idea is not automatically equal to great results. Resist being average at all times. I worked in an after-school program in Southeast, DC, when the Let's Move! campaign launched. It was a White House initiative with the mission to provide more healthy lunch options in public schools. Schools began serving foods such as salmon, green vegetables, different kinds of pastas, and various fruit selections. So, I ask, did the mission achieve its goal? Yes, it did. There were more healthy lunch options in public schools. Unfortunately, the "solution" was a product of oversimplifying the problem therefore leading to shallow planning and execution, which leads to mediocre results. We must ask the tough question— did the campaign realize its purpose? No, it did not. I saw those students throw that food in the trash, every day, over and over. We can't simply replace a "bad thing" with a "good thing" and think that people are just going to adapt to it. Change only occurs with a multifaceted approach; however, a multifaceted approach involves above-average thinking, planning, and execution. While the idea was formed with great intentions and with an ideal social impact mission, the architects of the Let's Move! campaign ignored several critical structural problems. First, students' families weren't included in the movement. Efforts to educate families on the benefits of eating that type of food were minimal at best. Second, there was no attempt to consider whether families could continue the change at home. Could they afford to buy salmon? Many could not. And third, no one considered whether families had access to that type of food in their neighborhood, since each of those schools was in a food desert, where there were no grocery stores with fresh fruits and vegetables and fresh lean meats. The barriers to adopting healthy eating at home were immense. If we want to solve the unhealthy school lunch problem, then we should start with tackling the food desert in which the school is located. Campaigns such as this do not come from a place of relationship building, they are simply prescriptive. They are indeed mediocre solutions to complex problems. Solutions that might make us feel good, but feeling good doesn't solve real problems. The real work, the real solutions require building relationships with the people who will be most affected by the decisions corporations and politicians make. Here's the thing: complex problems only get solved when we do the work, the hard work, that is required of each of us. In the same way, the venture capital funding space must ask more nuanced questions. The mediocre outcomes are not an indication of being a mediocre person. We don't always get it "right" all of the time. I am sure that the Let's Move! campaign was very effective in some cities. You are allowed to try something big and dreamy. What you learn is what you earned from the experience. Invest the learning you earned into solving the problem better to avoid mediocrity.

In Chapter 1, you might remember that I received a note from a heterosexual white male on the Bumble dating app in which a man posted the comment: "If I started an organization called 'White male ventures,' you'd go apeshit." While you know how I leveraged this comment into a major partnership, his comment is a perfect example of the nuances of racial narratives in this country that are normalized and often internalized by Black and Brown people. Of course, his use of the term "ape" was particularly salient, given the historical racial trope of referring to Black people as apes. That aside, he's actually correct in that we don't need an organization called "white male ventures" because when you're a member of the dominant class, you don't need a qualifier, such as *African* American, *Latin* American, or *Asian* American, or even entrepreneur vs. *woman* entrepreneur. White Americans are simply known as "Americans," and venture capital for white males is just called "venture capital." White and male is the American default character for everything we do, and it divides all of us into categories and encourages us to compete for a slice of the dwindling proverbial pie.

In order to address the nuances of our narratives, consider the intersectionality of the structural identities of race, class, gender, and sexuality, and the interlocking systems of power and oppression. Intersectionality is not an explanation of personal identity. It is a description of power. So when I talk about having all perspectives at the table, I'm talking about the table of decision making. I'm not talking about the lunchroom table, or the break room table, not even necessarily the WeWork table in the coworking space, or in the coworking area of your office. The move toward diversity and equity does not stop with the presence of single individuals. It must go beyond that to address the larger structural obstacles to equality. Discrimination is baked in the cake of our national experience—baked into the structures of race, gender, and sexuality through our laws, culture, beliefs, and even our implicit associations. Dismantling this structure requires above-average work that far too many aren't willing to do. Even the "good guys" would rather create diversity quotas instead of implementing deep change. The needed change requires people to be exceptional, not mediocre.

These associations make up the reality of venture capital as well, and it is why you must resist being average in order to be successful in this space. To resist being average you must not only understand the nuances of equity, but you must do the hard work of creating and running above-average businesses that are the result of thinking outside the box. These types of businesses do not come up with average solutions to complex problems; these types of businesses start with understanding that the power is in the relationships you build with the people you are serving. The old industrial model of being a cog in a wheel at Ford Motor Company is gone, and this is a new age where the ones who rebel against mediocre solutions to complex problems will win. We cannot keep doing things the old way and hoping for different results. Problems will not get solved in today's world with employees who do the same repetitive tasks over and over again. Your company needs employees who do above-average work for a company that has created a solution that involves relationships with the people it serves. Had I understood these nuances when I began BGV early on, I could have been more effective at challenging the male Eurocentric default way of thinking that I bumped into over and over. At this point, I hope it is clear that the contents of this book should be carefully considered when you enter the world of venture capital fundraising, because you can't pioneer your own path to capital if you don't understand the fundamental nuances of the rules and how the rules have changed. Acknowledge the discrimination you will face, speak out against it, protest, do whatever it is you need to do, but don't let it be the reason you give yourself to resist starting a business. Don't let it be an easy reason for you to give up. Or a reason for you to do average work in the face of complex problems.

While the intersectionalities of our structural identities come together in overlapping ways to restrain the individual's ability to fully participate in our democracy, they also overlap in such a way that we can use them to create an equitable power structure, one in which we think more systemically about solving discriminatory practices and behaviors. For example, when we think about creating an equitable power structure, we don't have to plan how we'll have every single individual that represents every single identity in America at the table. Instead, we should think about the systematic process of introducing change. Cultural change should be introduced in the same way that new marketing campaigns are unveiled—strategically planning and methodically tagging, tracking, and labeling responses in order to inform the next decision. We have to stop and ask, "If we want to change or shift the culture, how do we roll this out thoughtfully? What will a shift in the power structure mean for everyone?" DEI does not only mean there are more diverse people at your proverbial table of power but also that their thoughts weigh heavily in the decision-making process.

Large, influential institutions that have focused only on the simplest form of meeting the diversity imperative—simply adding numbers of diverse people to previously excluded spaces—have tried to convince us that the nuances of our identities are too exhausting. The very people prescribing these solutions are often mediocre, yet they have been told that they are exceptional. That's a dangerous smoke screen. "You mean we need every representative of every group at the table, not just Black and white people, but a physically challenged person, and also people from different ethnicities, and women?" Then they move to the farcical: "Do we need people who can't spell too?" Finally, they decide that "we can't possibly have everybody, there's no way. But if we hit a certain percentage of right, it will be fine." Again, a mediocre way of thinking. You need to resist being average to succeed today in the face of structural isms as well as on your journey to building an amazing business that solves real-world issues.

A company with the attitude that it can't possibly address all nuances is solely focused on numbers—they're looking through the single lens of diversity. While single lens diversity promotes the importance of individual differences, diversity and inclusion focuses on creating a culture of respect, value, and belonging for all. Further, diversity and equity focus on addressing the unique barriers that disadvantage any subgroup of people. This example of mediocre thinking and solutions can be applied to any problem we are seeking to solve today, including the problems you might be facing in your business right now.

Understanding these nuances will help you challenge corporations and corporate leaders who are truly thinking about their bottom line and will get them thinking about how they're going to make more money, how to create economic development, and about the quickly shifting demographics of this country where the majority of working-age individuals are people of color. They will have no choice but to come to understand that if they want to maintain their power, then they'd better figure out how to work with more people. The lack of diversity and equity in our power structures is a foundational problem that no one diversity investment plunged into a long history of oppression is going to change. If a company is truly dedicated to making more money and building a strong business, then looking at DEI as a loss of power doesn't make sense. When you broaden your reach to more people, your power expands.

To give another example, the same problem happens in the educational system: treating every student in the public school system the same is an average way of thinking, which doesn't solve the complex challenges the school system faces. Because what happens when you have an exceptionally smart student or a student who is below average? Well, then we have a problem because the system can't meet these students' needs. Which is the tragedy of standardized tests and even teachers who want to do above-average work within a system that is forcing mediocrity on them.

Power is a relationship. It's not something that can be taken, or even given. It's not like pie. There aren't just so many slices. Power expands and contracts depending on how we use it. Power is something that is negotiated. Let this be a reminder that you have the power to create something that is better than average, if you are willing to resist being average and come up with solutions that are not easy but that actually prioritize solving problems with people in mind. Do the work to resist being average, and in the long run you will create a business that has far greater impact on the people you serve than simply settling for mediocrity along the way.

Dig Deeper to Build Taller

If you build on shaky foundation, you will always be under construction. I grew up in a middle-class home with a strong foundation of support and family. But when I was in ninth grade, that stereotypical middle-class structure—traditional Christian mother and father, two kids, and a dog living within a white picket fence surrounding a perfectly manicured lawn— began to overwhelm me. I saw no room to imagine something different for my life. There was no room to conceive of what the intersections of my identity could look like in experience. I'm queer, I'm Black, I'm a woman, and at that time I wanted to be an entrepreneur, and to push and poke at the boundaries of possibility. I rebelled against the rules required to live that middle-class lifestyle. But without a tether to some type of ideal way to be to grasp onto, I fell onto very shaky ground, and my life spun out of control. For many of us, we were taught to fit in. To want a life that isn't right for us. Our parents, wanting the best for us, wanted us to fit in. Go to school, get a good job and follow the rules—that's average. However, we can see now—more than ever—that the script we have been conditioned to follow is making a lot of people unhappy. Living a life that requires us to do the same work, every day, from nine to five without an outlet to express our creativity or solve problems doesn't work for a lot of people. Society wants us to fall in line because that's how we keep the system going, but what happens when you resist being average? I know the thought is scary, but on the other side of that fear the life you really want might just be waiting for you. And it might look completely different than the image society has sold you.

Years ago I found myself in a relationship with a man who not only refused to support my dreams but also actively sought to persuade me to give them up and get a traditional job. I considered acquiescing to what he wanted. I thought, *I could stay here, I could try to work it out with this man who is not good for me. I could try to tinker with this layer, or I could just knock this whole thing down and do something else.*

When I refused him, he left me with three children to care for on my own, and the cost of living became my enemy. The cost of living says you can't afford to live as a single person in the United States with three children. In order to survive, I accessed all of the resources available to my family from our society, like the free lunch program at school and food stamps. *And* I thought about what skills I had. It's important to do both simultaneously. You can't be creative when you're worried about feeding your children. But just because you get help to feed your children, it doesn't mean you stop there. So I asked myself, "What skills do I have? Can I build something? Can I paint something? Can I perform something?" At that point, it was all about what I *did* have, not what I *didn't* have, and not what I lost.

The second lesson I learned from building my shoe tower was that in order to have a stable structure, the depth of my foundation has to equal the height of my tower. I was watching a random show once about how skyscrapers are built, and the builder said, "If you want to build tall, the first thing you do is dig deep."

Take, for example, our nation's work-around equity and inclusion. We have built as tall as we have dug so far, and now things are crumbling. But we keep fiddling with the top of the structure. By that I mean we keep tinkering with the last batch of hires we made, the last system we created. But we need to dig to the root causes of inequity and exclusion to understand how to build a stronger foundation for the long term. And that requires work. Above-average work. It requires a complete overhaul of the system. And as we all know, no one likes change. It's easy to keep doing the same thing in the same way, even if there is a better way to do it. That way of thinking is not good enough if you want to run a great business.

When I called off my engagement, I had to dig deep within myself to find the courage to say, "Okay, I don't know what we're going to do, but I'm going to do something, and this time I'm not going back. I'm not going back."

The third shoe tower lesson came from the Intelligent Fast Failure (IFF) concept about the frequency and intensity of failures to measure improvement. So my motto is "fail fast and fail smart." Failure is inevitable. In almost everything we do, there will be aspects that we could do better. But to ensure that those failures—whether big or small—lead to better performance, we must fail intelligently, recognize quickly when something isn't working, and be willing to let it go and try something else. That's the beauty of entrepreneurship. It is all about failing and getting better. For most people in a typical nine-to-five job, they are not failing; they are doing the same work every day without fail. So they are not growing, they are a cog in the wheel. As an entrepreneur you have the ability to create and run a business that transforms people's lives, and you have the ability to do things better for the people you employ. Resisting being average, resisting building an average business, also means resisting hiring average employees.

On my journey, I built several businesses, none of which brought in the revenue my family needed and therefore did not create stability. Each time, however, I learned something important that I could use the next time. For example, when I launched my t-shirt business, a friend told me to take them in bulk to conferences and sell them. It sounded like a solid idea. But that friend had never started a business. And while the advice sounded good, it was disastrous. First of all, I had to expend capital up front to purchase t-shirts in bulk, then I had to transport the product back and forth to conferences, but I ended up selling a minuscule number of shirts. The cost significantly outweighed the benefit. I learned a very important lesson: if you have not built a successful business, I'm not interested in or open to your feedback.

With each failure, I considered the concept of IFF. I could either tinker with those businesses or knock them down and say, "What's next? What can I build that will stand?"

After five attempts, I came upon my first successful business—a print shop. When I developed Ms. Print USA, I established a business model that was built on relationships. And it worked!

I finally created stability for my family. But I didn't stop there. My next endeavor was Black Girl Ventures Foundation, and I used all the social currency that I had built with the print shop as a foundation for this next layer.

I reached a point of realization right before launching BGV. I had done everything that I could do to get myself to a certain point—like just hustling hard and harder to get where I wanted to be in life—but in order to move beyond that point I had to become strategic. You can't successfully pioneer a path to sustainability without strategy. To reach a level of sustainability, you have to go bigger than the grinding fast-paced moment-to-moment hustle of daily survival.

Digging deep is like taking a deep breath before blowing up a balloon. You take that deep breath, release the initial blow, and fill that balloon to the first level. Next, in order to expand the balloon, you take another deep breath and release. Then continue that process until the final breath, which brings you to the place where you tie the knot in the stem—that is the place of stability, that is the place where you can be what Seth Godin calls a linchpin. Seth Godin is a marketing guru and author of 18 books. He is famous for his marketing strategies and his ability to create a buzz around any product or service. According to Godin, a true linchpin is indispensable to a business, they make things happen, they do not need a manual. They have the ability to make decisions and create value. They can move an organization in the right direction without having to be told. That means you need to create an indispensable product that is important enough to enough people, and you need to hire employees who are linchpins. This mindset is the way to the top and the way to change culture and disrupt systems.

Resist Average Hires

You should hire people who are passionate about what they do and who are willing to go the extra mile in their work. The average CEO wants to hire people who can follow rules, people who are easily replaceable. However, working with people who are easily replaceable results in people doing average work following a strict set of rules. In reality working with and hiring people who think outside of the box and are free to express themselves results in a win-win for the employee as well as the company.

Nonprofits such as BGV are required to have a board. The board is responsible for overseeing the organization's activities and ensuring that it is fulfilling its mission. The board is an integral part of the organization and is usually made up of people that have been chosen for their expertise and for what they can contribute to the organization. It's important that the board has a good mix of members from inside and outside the organization so as to ensure proper oversight. This mix also ensures the board has the necessary expertise to make important decisions, as well as bringing in fresh perspectives and insights. Here's the thing: nonprofit boards are a great way to give back to the community and make a difference. They are also a great way to network with other people in the same field. As a board member, nonprofit boards are not just about giving money; they also require time and effort. It is important for board members to be committed and show up for meetings. I had a board chair that is above-average— exceptional even. Kristina, a former employee of Booz Allen, which is an American management and information technology consulting firm that provides consulting, analysis, and engineering services to public and private sector organizations and nonprofits. We developed a really tight relationship.

My board chair didn't work in the business day-to-day, but when it came to funding or brainstorming I can bounce things off her. We can talk about everything. We can talk about intuition, how you use intuition around a business, and how you lean into your intuition. This is an above-average person with whom I have an above-average relationship beyond the typical board chair role. It was my board chair who first told me, in passing, that one day we would work with Nike. This is also true for the advisors on my board.

Advisors should have industry-specific expertise. I always tell people, "I don't care if you launch a basket weaving company, you still should have somebody on your advisory board that specializes in baskets or wicker or making containers out of wood." You want people who have industry-specific expertise as advisors. You can meet these types of people at trade conferences, but as we discussed in Chapter 5, finding board members or even employees requires you to use L.I.A. (linkage, interest, and ability). You should not only be thinking about L.I.A. in terms of getting funding but in all areas of relationship building from hiring coaches to consultants to advisors and friends.

Alex, one of my advisors, has been pivotal in thinking outside the box in terms of developing BGV. A friend of mine invited me to an investing gathering. It was a small, intimate group of people there. At the event people were saying over and over again that there was "plenty of money" in Washington, DC. After about the fifth time hearing this, I couldn't take it anymore. I raised my hand because I'm a hand raiser. That's what I do. So to all my hand raisers out there, I got you. At any rate, trying to figure out how to be very diplomatic about it, I said, "I understand, you know, there's money around here.

I get it, but can you help me understand where it's going because less than 1% of Black women have access to capital?" I went on to tell them that when they say, "There's plenty of money out here," they are really referring to a small group of white people. This was a jarring comment to the room. Especially because it was a room of well-meaning, progressive white people. They seemed genuinely shocked that the money wasn't going to people of color. Alex was at this event, but we hadn't known each other at this point. He commented that people in that room hadn't even had to think about the disparity in funding and that it was a good thing to think about. I made a mental note from his comment, and we exchanged information. Alex later reached out to me to set up a meeting. Just to talk. I met with him several times and was able to hear his perspective on a wide range of topics. During these meetings with Alex, gender or race didn't matter because we both recognized that there was a challenge here and his perspective on that challenge is what aligned with my objective to change the world. This made him a viable candidate to be an advisor for BGV. Which is a reminder that mediocre people can't see past identity, and I don't need mediocre people on my board or as employees. Alex helped BGV build out and launch this idea for a donor advisor fund during the pandemic. The donor advisor fund is a vehicle that allows us to invest in BGV alumni. It is not a traditional venture capital fund where you get a return in your pocket, but with this fund the return goes back to the donor advisor fund. Alex has also connected us to a business developer to help BGV raise money. Alex is exceptional. He goes above and beyond. Let me be clear, above-average people do not say things like "That's not in my job description."

Activate Your Social Capital

In Chapter 5 we talked about building relationships through linkage, interest, and ability. The ideal opportunity for a constructive relationship will hit the linkage-interest-ability trifecta. But what about relationships where you have two out of three? For example, someone may be interested in the same issues as you and have the ability to help, but you may not have any link to them. Is this relationship worth pursuing?

First and foremost, this should be seen as an opportunity to find a link. Do some research into their past, their present, their passions, their predicaments, and see if there is anything you can find to connect with them on a more human level. But if you exhaust everything and don't find any inroads, you will have to weigh where you are in your business's journey and what other opportunities you have available to you. If there are more promising avenues to pursue, prioritize those; if there aren't, consider the potential upside and downside and which factors are most useful to you where you are right now. Being thoughtful about the people and organizations you involve in your journey will make sure you are spending your energy where it can do the most good. The real question is, how do you activate your social capital? The answer is to play your cards right. Remember the four suits. You know how to determine if a relationship is a real opportunity, and how to make inroads with the people in question. As you are building your network, how do you figure out what resources you have and how to organize them intentionally? To simplify things, let's create a taxonomy of connections based around the four card suits: hearts, spades, diamonds, and clubs. There are different types of people in your network.

Hearts—the Believers

The hearts are the believers. These are the people who believe in your cause and follow your journey closely and give you their time and support without asking for anything in return, simply because they believe in you and your work. You may feel reluctant asking for volunteers when you need them, but these are the people who will volunteer to help you anyway. To keep these people an active part of your network, feed them content. They are interested in your progress, so they will wait for news, and they will read and talk about and share what you post and have feelings in response. For example, consider the power of the diehard fan community of popular YouTuber MrBeast. His fan base originated and boosted the idea for his "Team Trees" project via social media; in celebration of reaching 20 million YouTube subscribers, MrBeast successfully raised $20 million within two months for the Arbor Day Foundation. Twenty million new trees are being planted as a result. As this illustrates, keep the believers in the loop by feeding them content, and they will be your biggest supporters and open unexpected new doors for you. The believers are liking, following, cheering you on, and volunteering to help. Be sure to feed the believers. Be sure that they have things to react to in order to stay connected to you or your company.

Spades—the Linchpins

The spades are the linchpins. These are people who are on the same journey as you and dealing with many of the same hurdles you are dealing with. They may be a couple of steps ahead of or behind you, but these are people living in your world who you may admire and want to work with. To activate this group of people, collaborate with them. These are people who are leading and creating, who are asking questions and discussing and pushing forward their own goals and values. Finding the right linchpins and collaborating with them at the right times can create a synergy between your goals and help everyone involved. For example, consider the partnership between Black Girl Ventures and Black Ambition, a nonprofit founded by Pharrell Williams to close the opportunity and wealth gap for Black and Latinx entrepreneurs. The CEO is Felecia Hatcher, a multi-hyphenate serial entrepreneur, coach, and speaker. I met Felecia about three years into building BGV. We would see each other at conferences, trade advice, and swear we would find time to work together or to just hang out. We were both head down working to change the world. How would we ever find time to work together? Text messaging has been our way of keeping in contact. When she has a thought or challenge I may have insight on she sends a text. When I am stuck whether it's confidence or founders and funders I reach out to her. We are careful with each other's time. As she has developed Black Ambition into the powerhouse social impact effort it is today, she has kept me in mind for opportunities. In 2021, I created Pull Up & Pitch, a pop-up style pitch competition that funds entrepreneurs and small business owners in real time at live events. Entrepreneurs pitch for 60 seconds to three judges who will give them a thumbs up or thumbs down. If they receive one thumbs up, they will receive $200, two thumbs up gets them $250, and three thumbs up gets them $500 and a chance to go to the second round to pitch for up to $20,000 as well as mentoring and more perks. When Pharrell decided to bring back his music festival "Something in the Water" in 2021, the Black Ambition team reached out to partner on having Pull Up & Pitch at the event. It was a huge success. The line to pitch was stretched down the street. Pharrell also came over to visit the activation. The top seven founders received an opportunity to pitch to him. The key to working with linchpins is alignment and timing. Pull Up & Pitch meets the impact needs of both Black Girl Ventures and Black Ambition. It fulfills the mission that Felecia and I are on. The alignment and timing made it easy for us to work together this way to create the change we want to see in the world. The linchpins are just as busy as you are. Consider them for partnerships that allow them to activate in their zone of genius on your behalf.

Diamonds—the Champions

The diamonds are the champions. These are people who are out in the world spreading your message and proselytizing on your behalf while you are hard at work. They showcase your work to those unfamiliar with it and testify to your skill, and they urge others to work with you and warn them not to miss out. To activate the champions, all you have to do is empower them to run with your story. Whenever your story has a new update, like when your brand or experience or mindset changes, make sure to clue the champions in and give them the new ammunition to fight your battles with. These people are already on your side, so don't hold them back. Champions are behind the word-of-mouth success of all kinds of endeavors, from book series such as *Harry Potter* and *Twilight* to TV shows such as *Squid Game*. But maybe the most classic example of the power of champions is Jesus' apostles. As miracle follows miracle, the apostles spread the Gospel to strangers and nonbelievers. Regardless of your religious beliefs, the apostles give us a great insight into the impact that a few people who believe in your message and go out and communicate it to the world can have. Share with your diamonds. Be sure they know what to champion about you or your company.

Clubs—the Gatherers

The clubs are the gatherers. These are the organizers, the people who already believed in the same values and goals you are working toward independently of your involvement. They convene and charge and collaborate and townhall about this topic, and as such they have the power to help you scale your work when it intersects with their goals. To activate the gatherers, engage them. When you are ready to expose your work to a large group of people and cause a large reaction, drop it into a group of gatherers. Keep a list of gatherers so that when you need to, you can create a big impact. Activist groups are a great example of this structure. For example, the Black Lives Matter organization regularly highlights smaller and more local causes in the wake of high-profile events, such as fundraisers for protestors' legal fees or petitions for justice for individual victims of police brutality. Another example is the nonprofit Foundation to Decrease World Suck, led by brothers John and Hank Green. This organization raises money for philanthropic purposes and then distributes this capital equitably among various charities as chosen by the community surrounding the organization, allowing those charities to greatly scale their outreach and funding. Package and share with the clubs. They are already engaged in your industry, and they already have an affinity for your type of product or services. When you are ready to scale, the clubs can be an important part of the word spreading fast and efficiently.

To make use of these structures, find the people who share your aims and ideals and then engage them to allow you to help each other.

Bonus Group—the Jokers

The jokers are a bonus group. These are people who are wealthy and connected and have much wider reach and influence than you. These are the people who can fund your business and open doors for you if you play your cards right. The jokers are very useful in your journey—if you involve them at the right time. The key is to involve them once you are very clear on exactly what you are setting out to do, how you will get there, and what you need from them to bridge that gap. These players are themselves looking for certain signals in the people they meet to determine if you are the right partner for them. If you involve them when you are still figuring things out, you will be missing these qualities, and you will be passed over because you aren't bringing anything to the table. Funding is important, but purpose and value is the priority. Money won't solve disorganization, so build your business and build your network, and soon enough you'll be in a position where you're offering as much value as you are getting.

The key to all of these types of relationships is that a transactional relationship is an unhealthy relationship. Transactions happen as a by-product of an authentic relationship where you share goals, values, and camaraderie with people. Not all professional relationships have to evolve into personal ones, of course, but try to look beyond what someone can do for you in a narrow sense and look at the bigger picture. Try to connect with them as real people who have entered your orbit because you share a common experience, and your network will run both wide and deep. My challenge for you is to resist being average. Identify above-average people and make genuine connections on a human level. Once you can do this, you can then activate your social capital in a more meaningful and intentional way.

PART III

Innovate

CHAPTER 7

Intuitive Decision Making

The Journey Is Real

When I first moved to the DMV area, I got a job working in the logistics office of DHL coordinating trucks and handling other similar duties. I had applied to a job at the patent trademark office with no luck, while one of my best friends from college had gotten a job offer for the patent trademark office. I couldn't figure out what I had done wrong. Seeing my frustration, he spoke to the hiring managers on my behalf; thanks to his intervention, the hiring managers took an interest in me and asked me to send over my resume—once again showing the value of having a champion in your corner. My friend came over to my mom's house and helped me update my resume, and then I emailed it to them.

Days went by and turned into weeks, and still I heard no response. I started feeling antsy again, seemingly having been rejected by the same team twice, but I put it out of my mind—until, one night, I had a dream. In my dream, I found I had misspelled a word in the email I sent to the group of hiring managers. When I woke, I dismissed the thought as silly, but over the next couple of days the sense that something was amiss kept nagging at me, until I finally decided to give in and check the email I had sent.

Sure enough, I had misspelled a word.

Even though it was weeks later by this point, I rewrote the sentence and sent off a follow-up email—"I just realized that I misspelled a word in this email. I wanted an opportunity to correct it." To my surprise, they emailed me right back and asked me to come in for a job interview. I landed the job.

While this chain of events may seem like an unbelievable stroke of pure luck for me, it's not. It's actually a direct result of a force that's operating in all of us at all times: intuition.

Intuition is the everyday superpower, the sixth sense, the guiding hunch in the back of your head. Intuition is not logical. It is not a balanced and thorough list of concrete pros and cons. Intuition is pure knowing. It is our connection to forces larger than ourselves, whether that is God, the universe, or just each other. It is what you know to be true in your heart when faced with questions that logic alone can't answer.

Notice I said heart. People often call your intuition a "gut feeling," but I think the heart is a more apt metaphor, because it runs on autopilot, is constant, and gives life to all things. A lifetime of experience and wisdom pushing us invisibly through life fuels those feelings in our heart that tell us when to grab hold of an opportunity and when to let it pass us by. It holds a subtle power that can't be named but can be seen everywhere.

But you don't have to take my word for it; Steve Jobs is quoted in his self-titled biography as saying, "Intuition is a very powerful thing, more powerful than intellect, in my opinion." This is a credible statement coming from a man whose vision and branding famously revolutionized the tech industry by foreseeing what the public wanted before they even had the imagination to want it. His intuition is what allowed him to ignore the naysayers and "know" better. Similarly, in an interview published in *The Saturday Evening Post* in 1929, Einstein reportedly said, "I believe in intuitions and inspirations. I sometimes feel that I am right. I do not know that I am." Einstein's numerous scientific contributions to the field of physics were driven in large part by imagination and intuition;

in particular, Einstein's theory of special relativity was born of a thought experiment considering how a beam of light would appear to an observer traveling alongside it through a vacuum at the speed of light. While the accepted laws of physics at the time suggested that the beam of light would appear to be an electromagnetic field at rest, Einstein intuited that this felt wrong, and revolutionized science as we know it in the process. And then there is Oprah Winfrey, who has made a career of her instinctive ability to connect with others and get them to open up emotionally. She says, "I've trusted the still, small voice of intuition my entire life. And the only time I've made mistakes is when I didn't listen. It's really more of a feeling than a voice—a whispery sensation that pulsates just beneath the surface of your being. All animals have it. We're the only creatures that deny and ignore it."

Personally, I came to my belief in the still, small voice of intuition from growing up in the Pentecostal church. In a world where the Holy Spirit takes hold of people and preachers laying hands on you have the power of divine healing, the belief of being connected to something beyond yourself and being pulled to goodness by the invisible hand runs deep. Trusting the feeling that comes from the preacher laying hands on me taught me to believe that there must be some muscle that the preacher has exercised to get that level of connectivity to God.

My first real testing ground for building intuition came from my experience performing poetry. On the advice of a woman I met through blog talk radio—where I had only ever performed my poetry with no visible audience—I attended my first open mics at Busboys and Poets in Shirlington, Virginia. This was my first opportunity to perform my poetry for an audience, and one who loved art at that, which was a blessing. I found that my poems were receiving polite applause, but they weren't getting anywhere near the huge reactions that other, more experienced poets were getting. I wanted my poems to resonate with and move people the way others' poems were, so I decided to set that as a goal and continue writing poems and returning every Monday to achieve that.

I recognized quickly that I was facing an uphill battle. The audience was majority white and middle class, and ironically I felt that the similarity between my middle-class upbringing and theirs—which should help me relate and resonate with them more—actually made my poetry less powerful in this setting, at least on a surface level. Because of my privilege of having two present parents with stable jobs and a seemingly idyllic life, I didn't have the obvious hardships that a lot of the other poets had. So I focused on what I could control: the mechanics and craft of poetry.

I worked long and hard to figure out how I could leverage what I was saying to actually create an impact on the people who were listening. Finally, one day I went back with a poem— I don't remember the exact poem, but I believe it was either about my grandmother or about getting pregnant as a teenager—and I got the reaction I had been looking for from the audience. I realized that people didn't need to have the same story as you; they just needed to be able to resonate with how you felt about whatever you went through. Once that lesson clicked for me, it was like a switch had flipped. From then on, I could do it easily; I could get to the bottom of my own story, and I could tell it in a way that would draw people to it. It was just a matter of what I call "running the reps," or repeatedly refining your process by engaging in it over and over again until it reaches your level of satisfaction.

Through this slow and meticulous process of practice and trial and error, I had developed an intuition for how to communicate my own story and how to use my words to create the effect I wanted to have on people in real time. As an engineer, I had learned to program computers with zeros and ones to get a desired result, and here I was learning to do the same with humans using sentences and emotions. This skill has of course served me well ever since and will serve you well if you work to develop it.

Skipping the hard work isn't an option, but the blessing of intuition is you have to obtain it and train it for yourself. Because intuition and instinct operate at a level beyond logic and discrete data, they can't be condensed and transferred to someone else. They have to be won through experimentation and experience. In other words, I can't give you my intuition; I can tell you how I have become in tune with my own and how you can listen to the voice inside you effectively. However, the journey to mastering your intuition is yours alone. It starts with a belief that this force is real and is there to guide you toward making decisions that will help you achieve becoming the best version of yourself. That may not be the advice or instruction you were looking for as I know the human brain wants a road map. This is the part of the book that doesn't make prescriptions because it has less to do with logic and more to do with spiritual law. I want you to view this as exciting though as this is what makes intuition magical. In the same way that you can't take anyone else's intuition, no one can take yours. Once you embrace the power of your intuition it has positive implications across every area of your life. These include, but are not limited to, how to communicate and what you value, how to pick the right goals and make the right decisions to reach them, how to collaborate with and lead people, and how to thrive and excel in your lane. Intuition building is the thing that makes you undeniable. Intuition is the one competitive advantage that other people cannot take from you. Your logic, circumstances, and resources are all things that you can teach or show others, but your instinct is something you earned the hard way through trusting your inner voice and the spirit. It is the unexplainable foundation of your expertise. So, really, it's good news for you that I can't do that work for you. Are you ready to unlock a new world of possibilities, results, and outcomes? Are you ready to blow through that ceiling that has been holding you back? If so, keep reading.

How to Trust Intuition

Trusting your intuition is a slow process and begins with experimentation and self-awareness. The most forgiving way to begin training your sense of intuition is to first begin to notice the instincts you already have. Do you ever make decisions despite having a hunch that they are not the right way to go and then later beat yourself up saying things like, "I *knew* I shouldn't have done that," when those decisions don't work out? These moments can be anything, from "I *knew* I should have grabbed that umbrella" or "I *knew* I should have taken a different route to work," to "I *knew* I shouldn't have trusted that person" and "I *knew* I shouldn't have taken that job." Whatever they may be, take note of them as they happen, as they can give you a sense of what listening to or ignoring your intuition can feel like, as well as in which areas your intuition is already well trained and leading you in the right directions.

As you start to notice when your intuition is in motion, and as you begin trusting yourself to take bigger risks and test your hunches more, you can work through other exercises to calibrate your intuition. One that I learned from an intuition coach that I worked with is the "Body as a pendulum" exercise. This is a way to learn to recognize intuition acting in your body and use it to make decisions based on two points of feeling that you can identify with. Once you learn this exercise, you'll be able to rely on it anytime for the rest of your life.

To begin the exercise, sit quietly, breathe into yourself, and ground yourself. Let your mind, emotions, and body return to as neutral of a resting point as possible. Then, identify a person, place, thing, or experience that makes you feel a "Hell yes!" This can be anything that you are able to recall in your mind that makes you have a strong positive reaction, whether it's your favorite movie, seeing your kid smile, or in my case, hot air balloons. As you think about your "Hell yes," notice how your emotions and your body change and the feeling it sparks. Hopefully when you think about it, it makes you smile or laugh, and it makes you feel giddy and light. Sit with that feeling for a while, and then go back to neutral.

Then, think of something that makes you feel a "Hell no!" For me this is peas. I hate their mushy texture and don't know why they exist. For you this can be anything that gives you a strong negative reaction. Once you have it, sit with that feeling. You might notice your facial expressions starting to change and a frown or scowl coming over your face, or you might feel disgust or some other negative emotion elsewhere in your body. Take note of what that feels like.

Once you have calibrated the opposite ends of the spectrum with your "Hell yes!" and your "Hell no!" find the question you are struggling with the answer for. Make sure to frame the question as something specific, something that leans toward a bigger idea, and something that doesn't require logic to answer. These are the ideal types of questions to exercise your intuition. For example, "Is my boyfriend the one?" is too vague. The one what? Without further knowledge, there is no way to know. And "Should I leave my boyfriend?" doesn't connect to anything bigger than itself; you would have to weigh that against multiple criteria, and it would take a lot of logic and work to find that answer, and it may still not be possible. But a good version of the question might be, "Is my boyfriend the best fit for my long-term goals?" This is a tough question to answer with logic, since people change, circumstances change, and goals change, and there are a lot of factors to weigh, including the influence of your "rational" brain. But when you consider this question, you will hopefully have an immediate emotional reaction born from your intuition. Investigate that feeling and decide if it's closer to a "Hell no" or a "Hell yes" based on the poles we established previously. Another example of a good question might be, "Is getting an agent a good fit for my writing career goals?" It is possible that you won't have a strong emotional reaction to the question, which may mean that your decision doesn't actually have a strong impact on the question you are asking and it's up to you. Your intuition is there to steer you closer to your purpose—the best version of yourself. However, if the decision is a consequential one for your life, I encourage you to interrogate your feelings further and see if there are other thoughts blocking you from accessing your intuitive response. If you find that you still cannot access your intuitive response, the affirmation exercise outlined in Chapter 4 is worth revisiting here as it is the perfect solution. Remember, your intuition is the voice of your own inner wisdom and spirit speaking to you; to be able to hear it, you have to have the clarity to tune out other people's voices and your own ego and insecurities.

We can also turn to some tips from other experts to find more ways to build our intuition. Among other tips, Dr. Judith Orloff—MD, professor of psychiatry at UCLA, and author of *Dr. Judith Orloff's Guide to Intuitive Healing*—recommends paying attention to your energy levels. Whether a person or situation makes you feel drained or energized can tell you whether something is a good fit for you; "If you don't feel well around someone, your intuition is trying to tell you something," she says.

Dr. Orloff also recommends daily meditation, a tip seconded by Jack Canfield, coauthor of the *Chicken Soup for the Soul* series and *The Success Principles: How to Get from Where You Are to Where You Want to Be* among other works. "Regular meditation will help you clear your mind of distractions and teach you how to better recognize the subtle impulses from within," he writes. He also notes that even short meditation sessions can have profound effects. Canfield writes, "Even 10 minutes a day will yield powerful results and will make it much easier for you to notice your intuition when it speaks to you through words, images, emotions, or physical sensations." This matches Dr. Orloff's recommendation of a daily three-minute meditation routine, or even less if that's all that is possible.

Intuition Coaching

I mentioned earlier that I learned the "Body as a pendulum" exercise from an intuition coach, Shoshanna French. When I met her, I had just started BGV, but it was still in the very early days. I was in a period of my life where I was working hard on mental and spiritual self-improvement, but I had never heard of intuition coaching. I met this woman—a friend of a friend—at a party, and she introduced herself and explained what she did. They say that when a student is ready, the teacher will appear, and that's exactly what happened here. I had searched for a coach or mentor for a long time since I knew how important those relationships had been to the success of so many entrepreneurs, and here one had fallen into my lap. The only problem was that the entire coaching program cost $5,000, which was money I did not have, for the whole six-month program named *Mastering Intuition*. I had set a first goal for myself of earning $5,000/month, but at the time I was earning no money. At that point in my journey, something told me that I couldn't afford not to do it, so I scrounged together the money on a payment plan through substitute teaching, technical writing, and t-shirt sales, and I went through the program. And by the end of the six months, I had already gotten a contract for $5,000 a month from Google.

For me, the experience was absolutely worth it. The coach taught me to master deeper intuitive skills and awareness and how to apply them to life in a way that has been useful for me ever since. I believe in the content so much that I have also had my team trained on intuitive decision-making skills to empower them with tools to make decisions. I wanted them to be able to develop their own instincts for the right moves to make, whether it's for hiring and firing, partnerships, projects, or goals. Based on where you are in your journey, you will have to decide for yourself whether formal coaching like I pursued is right for you. There are plenty of intuitive coaches offering their services if you decide you want to go in that direction. But either way, the speed and magnitude of the changes this experience made for me should confirm the power of working on intuitive decision making in a dedicated way, so I highly recommend checking in with yourself often and using the exercises described in this chapter to build that muscle for yourself.

The power of intuition is that it captures knowledge and insight that we can't put into words any other way. The way we can feel someone watching us even without being able to see them, the way we know what ice cream flavor would really hit the spot right now, the way we know that someone gives us a sinking feeling that they're not as good a person as they seem—even if it operates in a place beyond visible logic, harnessing the power of those instincts can allow us to grow our business and reach our potential while dodging disaster along the way. Take some time to listen to the feelings in your heart and build that feeling of pure knowing every day, and you just might find answers coming to you in your dreams.

CHAPTER 8

Living at the Intersection of Multiple Things

When I began raising capital for Black Girl Ventures Foundation (BGV), one of the funders told me, "You're doing a lot. You're all over the place." I remember thinking, *Am I all over the place? I feel very focused, very clear on what I'm doing and the impact I intend to make.* But it wasn't clear to her because my journey to BGV didn't follow a traditional, simple, singularly focused path. Like most entrepreneurs, I have always lived at the intersection of multiple things. And if you're among that group of people, this chapter is dedicated to you.

At this intersection—where you may have had multiple careers or built multiple businesses or have been a person who works at a bank and sings or paints and cooks—you do more than one kind of job. You have more than one title, one profession, one way of earning a living, more than one way of being. And at this intersection you can pursue things that make you curious, things that fire you up, things that you're passionate about, or things that you simply see as necessary. At this intersection, you grow into the person you need to be to succeed in your business.

People like us, who frequently and persistently experiment with change, are often met with confusion from a society that promotes a narrow definition of career or job or financial stability—develop one expertise, become known as the go-to person for that expertise, and do it for the rest of your life. In doing so, your identity will become static, and that is the goal. For people like us, that goal crushes our spirit, our creativity.

In 2020, I changed my name. I added "Omíládé." Through a way-of-life custom that I practice I realized that I'm not the same woman my mother birthed, I have evolved into a new way of being. The name "Shelly" means "meadow on a ledge,"

"Omílàdé" means "the water that clears the path," and "Bell" is a sound that signals movement or a time of day. Together, the three characterize my identity as a person who leads interactions for others, makes a lot of noise to signal change, and has been trusted with the leadership they've acquired.

It took me a year to announce the change to the world, because those who only know one persona of me would have dismissed it. For them, I might be doing anything, anywhere, with anybody, and then without warning switch things around. For them, they would see the change as just a phase. "I don't know if I'm supposed to call her Omílàdé, because she'll move through that phase in another month or so, but everybody would've switched over, and now she's not doing it anymore." That is what they know of Shelly Bell.

That level of dismissiveness to shifts in growth and development becomes common when your identity isn't simple to comprehend, when it doesn't follow a traditional path. If other people can't get a clear understanding of who you are and what you do, then they feel that it's risky to do business with you. But other people's misunderstanding of you is not your responsibility, whether in business, career, personal relationships, or identities.

When I built BGV, I had a print shop. I sold T-shirts and printed for other people. I also did performance poetry and traveled up and down the East Coast. In addition to that, I studied computer science and taught middle school. So I know people who know me to be a poet, I know people who know me to be a teacher, I know people who know me to be a printer, and there are people who know me only because of what I do with Black Girl Ventures Foundation. At the intersection of all those industries is still just me. And what most will fail to comprehend or see is this: that intersection is where I learned to be an effective fundraiser.

In particular, being a poet helped me fundraise, because it taught me how to appeal to the human spirit by delivering my own story in an authentic way. I also learned to tell stories in a concise and clear manner. I learned the mechanics of running a print shop while I was a teacher, in the school's print shop. At the time I had no knowledge that years later I would launch a T-shirt shop, but the printing machine was there, and I thought it was cool, so I learned to print. When I decided to start a business, I thought, *I can start a print shop.*

When you have had the opportunity to engage in multiple experiences, you gain a deeper understanding of how to mitigate risk. You develop a strong emotional capacity to deal with crisis, like a lack of funds. You become resilient in figuring out how to overcome challenges. Founders with a one-pointed focus often come to me too afraid to launch their businesses. They have been doing one thing for so long that they lack the confidence to do anything else.

Take my children, for example. When my first son was old enough to start kindergarten, I had just graduated from college, and we moved to North Carolina. But just as he was about to transition to first grade, we moved to Maryland to live with my mother, and then within the year we moved again to Virginia. Between the end of first grade and the beginning of middle school, we moved so often that I thought, *This is not good. I'm moving my child around a lot.* So with my second son I was determined he would go to the same school from kindergarten to fifth grade, and to the same school from sixth grade to eighth grade. I had a dogged concentration on building what I thought was—or what society painted as—the picture of stability. As a result, my second son is significantly more risk averse than my oldest. My oldest son can flow with changes easily. As for my middle child, if we plan to go to the store and then decide to go at a different time, they are not happy at all. The entrepreneur must have a fluid mindset. The entrepreneur has to be able to navigate when the floor shifts unexpectedly, and the best trait a leader can have is self-awareness.

The successful entrepreneur also learns when to let go of things. T.D. Jakes tells a story about a man watching an eagle fly and admiring the grace and skill of the eagle. While in flight, the eagle swoops down and picks up a rodent of some kind. Suddenly, the eagle drops from the sky. The man goes over to investigate and finds the eagle dead. It had picked up a predator that scratched out its heart.

The question of when to hold on and when to let go has to be a personal one. Are you leading the thing, or is it leading you? Are you living the life you want, or are you coping with life? Who's in control, who is steering? If I'm the captain of my own destiny, do I have my hands on the steering wheel?

But letting go is not the same as giving up. Letting go is deciding what's working and what isn't. And it takes a hell of a lot of self-awareness to know what works for you, to know what is valuable, and to not confuse value with worth. Letting go is not an evaluation of your worth, because worth is related to cost, but value is a mutual exchange, a strategic determination of how a thing plays out for both parties, entities, or sides. Letting go characterizes the difference between value and worth. Analyze the value of what you're doing to determine whether to let it go or keep it.

When living at the intersection of multiple things, the questions you must ask yourself are, "Am I building a platform for myself to do multiple things?" or "Am I doing multiple things because I like to be busy?" If your goal is to build a platform as an expert on blah, then take all the things you've done and channel them through one avenue of expertise. But if your brain simply functions with more ease on multiple projects at once, that's also great. Do what makes sense for you. And while those are two very different questions, the answer can be yes to both.

When I started BGV, I landed on one thing. I didn't set out to do that, but it happened. I found my purpose. But my need for multiple things was also met under the umbrella of BGV. I can do everything I love. If I want to write and deliver a poem, I can do a poetry slam. If I want to have a retreat, I do it. If I want to have a live event, I do that. If I want to print T-shirts, I can print T-shirts. I get to be an artist and create, to be a tech entrepreneur and build platforms, and to go out into the community and talk to people. BGV does not take me away from the multiple things I love to do. It has provided an avenue for me to do what I love in a more secure and less risky way. I get to exercise all the parts of me through BGV. Here's the empowering thing about living at the intersection of multiple things: you have multiple talents that can serve you. This can be tricky though because you can easily get distracted or off-track if you don't develop healthy boundaries.

Don't Be Nice: Be Selfish

Living at the intersection of multiple things also means choosing yourself. Unfortunately, prioritizing choosing yourself and/or showing up for yourself is often called selfish—especially when it comes to being a woman. And women with children are definitely not supposed to choose themselves. I believe you can be there for yourself and your children, but even with your children you should have healthy boundaries. You cannot show up for yourself without embracing boundaries. It is not selfish to have boundaries. A big part of being a successful entrepreneur is being able to have boundaries as a business owner; otherwise, you'd never get anything done. A client, let's call her Jill, that I work with was sharing with me that she often runs into prospects that beg her to do one-on-one coaching calls. Jill runs a successful branding company, and a part of the program she runs includes coaching; however, Jill does not offer coaching unless an individual signs up for her premium program. When I asked Jill why she didn't want to offer one-off coaching or select coaching packages without the program her response was, "Because that's a distraction." When I asked her to explain, she said that she has a vision to help women of color level up their authority and income through branding, and there is a road map for doing that. The road map is inside her program, which she spent a year putting together. She has seen big results for clients who have trusted the process and enjoys coaching those clients along the way. She said if she started doing coaching outside the program, it would dilute her brand and damage her vision because those people outside the program wouldn't be able to get the comprehensive instruction they needed. Jill could just as easily charge additional clients thousands of dollars for coaching packages and take the money straight to the bank. However, Jill is clear on her purpose and has a vision that she has committed to. Jill has boundaries, and as a result she has a successful six-figure business that serves a niche area of the market.

People should stop telling women to be nice. No one ever tells men to be nice. What does being "nice" actually mean? Over the course of our lives as women we are repeatedly—and from a very young age—taught that we have to be nice, and in doing so we must also be selfless. As a result, women often find it impossible to grow, because we are so focused on ensuring that everyone else is taken care of.

When I was a child, I had big birthday parties. Fifteen or more of my friends would attend, and my mother would do all sorts of things—from roller-skating to bowling to swimming. It was just a really good time. We were girls being girls. Naturally, I would gravitate toward a friend that I liked more than others, or maybe there would be a couple of friends that I talked to more than others, and that made some of the girls angry.

I remember my mother saying, "You've got to be nice to everybody."

And I thought, *But it's my birthday!*

In retrospect, I wish my mother had said to those girls, "The point of Shelly's birthday party is so that everybody celebrates her. You can also play with the other little girls."

But what I wished for never happened. And that scenario has played out over and over and in various ways has affected my confidence in every area of my life, including hiring and managing my organizational team.

I have always wanted to create an environment where people can show up as themselves and share their thoughts. I strongly believe it's okay to disagree with one another.

In the early days of building BGV, I desperately wanted to be nice. I consistently found myself jumping in to do work that I shouldn't have been doing. I was so concerned about being nice that I didn't want to ask my employees to do too much. But as the CEO of a national organization, I was no longer the person who should be managing the administration of the organization. I was the leader. And I had to level up.

During those early days, while working with a particular contractor I received an excessively long email challenging the four priorities I had determined for her work with BGV.

My coach and I met to discuss my possible response. "I really just want to be nice," I said to my coach. She said to me, "It's not nice to let people walk all over you. The nicest thing you can do is to train people on how to treat you."

Being selfish is the confidence booster women need in order to find our place in a world where we have been conditioned to *just be nice*. This conditioning is in complete contradiction to the world of business.

Deciding to manage the expectations of others around you to meet your needs—while potentially appearing selfish—is really you standing up for yourself.

You are removing your ability to choose when you don't choose yourself.

Failing to manage expectation is not being nice, nor is it an act of selflessness. The question then becomes, "Are your values aligned with the way you're acting?"

Choosing yourself is about *leveling up*. It is about the feelings you experience when you're moving to different levels in your journey as you make different decisions about achieving your goals. Such decisions will require you to think in a way that others will likely see as selfish. As you take into account where you are and where you want to go, you may also have to change your environment, your friends, and your priorities. The more you embrace your ability and comfortability with living at the intersection of multiple things, the more changes you will have to make. There will always be adjustments to be made as you grow and step into the beautiful life you are creating for yourself. Always remember to be aligned with the changes you choose.

CHAPTER 9

Omí's Toolkit

The purpose of this book was to help you, the entrepreneur, level up your business and live the life of your dreams even in the face of adversity and naysayers. There are some things in this book that I've assumed you would know or understand how to incorporate into your business plan such as your vision statement or brand statement. There are tons of these types of tools online for you to choose from if you do not yet have those things. It's likely that you already have a well-defined mission, brand, vision, and purpose statement. It is also just as possible that you don't. This chapter is designed to help you learn some tactical skills that you can implement right now. Even if you already have some of these things in place, this chapter will give you the mindset to understand how to further construct the goals you want to accomplish so that you can live the life of your dreams. Notice I said construct. You have the power to program so many things in your life and the things in it. For many of us, this actually starts with reprogramming the scripts we've been told all of our lives.

One of the most beneficial skills I have acquired along the way is computer programming. During my undergraduate years, I was required to take lots of programming courses. Computer programming exercises show you that even in your everyday life you can program the things around you. Branding is programming. Your business marketing is programming. Your audience fundraising is programming. There is a program to talk to different types of funders, as we've already discussed in this book. By having a sound infrastructure internally, your company is programming its employees. You are literally programming everything around you. An exercise that I give to lots of people is to look at where you are in your room. Then write down step-by-step the instructions to get to the door. Write it as if you were a programmer. Computers don't know anything. When you see computers say, "Hey Kayla. . .," that's because you have programmed the name "Kayla" into your computer. Without algorithms computers can't do the complex things they do for us today. Computers cannot adapt to human behavior without any input. It's the reason we always have hiccups with computers. Computers and software need to be updated constantly because they can't easily contextualize. They are just good at following instructions. Think about your business as well as your current circumstances and analyze what instructions you are prescribing. When I say try to write instructions in your room to get from where you are to the door, what most people normally do is write down instructions with phrases such as "turn right" or "turn left." However, if those are the extent of your instructions, which seem logical at first, you will find that those types of directions will result in people spinning around and around, without really getting anywhere. If you tell a computer to turn, it's just going to turn without any guidance. You have to give more specific directions than that. You have to say things such as "turn 90 degrees" and "take 15 steps forward." You have to define every part of the motion that it takes to get to the door. That's why on our websites we still have to have buttons that say, "buy now," "shop here." Otherwise, people would lose interest, get confused, and ultimately not end up buying anything from us. People like to be told what to do, just like computers need to be told what to do. Customers are paying you because they want and need clear instructions on how to solve their problem. Human beings need guidelines to know what to do on your website. When it comes to running my business, I try to look at lots of things from my computer programming brain—everything is ones and zeros. I'm always looking at things in terms of cracking the code or creating the code to unlocking the door. Ask yourself, what systems does your business have in place? Are the systems programmed correctly? Are you giving directions that will lead to a positive result? What is your internal programming? What aspects of your conscious or subconscious do you need to reprogram in order to be successful?

Reprogramming Your Subconscious Mind

Dr. Bruce Lipton, a developmental biologist that bridges science and spirituality, discovered in his 40s that he needed to reprogram everything he had learned. As a cellular biologist, he had been a firm believer up to that point in the dominance of genetics in explaining all aspects of life. However, one fateful experiment changed his worldview for good.

While researching stem cells, Dr. Lipton observed a curious phenomenon: genetically identical stem cells placed in different environments developed into different types of cells. Stem cells derived from the same source placed in different Petri dishes would develop into fat, muscle, bone, and so on. The foundation of Dr. Lipton's belief system, that genes control life, began to show cracks. How could genes control life when the environment seemed to control the fate of cells with the same genes? This question began his journey in the field of epigenetics.

Epigenetics is the study of heritable changes that do not depend on the DNA sequence, and Dr. Lipton became convinced that it was the correct model for human behavior and life outcomes. He began sharing his findings with the world, along with the message that people could take control of their own lives by breaking free from the belief that they were doomed to a certain fate by their genes and instead realizing that their lives were a product of their beliefs. However, he was confronted by opposition pointing out that, for all of his teaching about the ability to reshape their lives as they please, he himself was not happy. At the time, he was going through a divorce with his first wife, had lost his father to cancer, and indicates that he was what many psychologists would call manic depressive.

Taking this criticism to heart, he decided to apply his teachings to his own life first, and he quickly transformed into a happy camper. Soon after, he wrote his book *The Biology of Belief* to share his story and his findings and has been a vocal proponent of epigenetics and the power of reprogramming your mind to improve your life.

The core tenet of Dr. Lipton's philosophy is that 95% of the time, our thoughts and actions are driven by our subconscious mind, which runs on autopilot using habits we learned accidentally long ago. He explains this by drawing an analogy to computers. "The brain is an information processor, a computer," he explains on Lewis Howes's podcast *The School of Greatness*. And just like a computer, the brain executes programs to accomplish most of its functions.

These "programs," running in the background, are what make up the subconscious mind, which is in control 95% of the time. The conscious mind is only in control the other 5% of the time, the same way your keyboard and mouse only control 5% of what happens on a computer. Unfortunately, because this 5% is what's most visible to us and what we see when we are focused and paying attention, we often ignore the programs at work the other 95% of the time.

So where do we get these programs from? Dr. Lipton emphasizes that it is not from our genetics or anything similarly immutable. Even in the case of disease, research now shows that, outside of a few outliers that have primarily genetic causes, genetic factors make up less than 10%—and often less than 5%—of the causative factors of diseases, including cancer. The vast majority of disease-causing factors are lifestyle and environmental factors.

Rather than receiving them from genetics, we primarily "download" these programs during the first seven years of our lives from the examples set by our family and, to a lesser extent, other authority figures (e.g. teachers, older siblings, extended family). Many of these programs can be good, for instance, being able to walk without thinking about it. However, many of these programs can also be bad, from unhealthy relationships with food and exercise to a poor relationship with money to unsuccessful interpersonal relationships to negative self-talk.

A study titled "How Infants and Young Children Learn About Food: A Systematic Review" published in the *Frontiers in Psychology* journal in 2017 found that children begin their lives totally dependent on their caregivers for their food needs and gradually move to autonomy by the age of three or four. They note that children begin their lives with very few inherent food preferences, and that "the environment—and the family home in particular—play a crucial role in shaping children's eating behaviors." They also posit that the eating habits established at this early age carry through the rest of the person's life and can have an impact on the probability of disease later in life.

Since these programs run our lives the vast majority of the time, the only way to redirect your life toward your goals is to reprogram your brain so that your subconscious and conscious minds are in harmony with each other.

Bruce tells the story of how he began to reprogram his brain, which began during one particular drive. He was driving in his car, stuck at a red light, and he realized he was going to be late. All of a sudden, he started berating himself, saying things like, "Well, you can't do things right. You're not good enough. You're an idiot." Noticing that his subconscious was inundating him with this negative self-talk, he interrupted this monologue and disempowered it by covering up the clock in his car. By being conscious of his subconscious programming for long enough to stop and address it, he was able to stop the barrage of insults, keep himself in a happy mood, and arrive at his destination right on time.

In another similar occurrence, Bruce recounts an experience in which he was setting up an experiment. This particular experiment required nearly two hours to set up and could only be run after that setup was done. Additionally, the experiment was very fragile; any small mistake could require starting over completely. On this day, Bruce was forced to set up and perform the experiment from scratch no fewer than three times, and each time it failed. By the end he was extremely frustrated, and his temper was flaring; once again he found himself criticizing himself relentlessly and becoming increasingly negative and upset.

However, on this occasion, he heard a different voice respond to the negative voice he usually heard; this new voice, as he explains on the Lewis Howes Podcast, said, "Don't you have anything better to do than to listen to this crap?" Bruce found this interjection from this new voice—the voice of his "higher self," as he describes it—hilarious. Agreeing, he picked up a newspaper, found a showtime for a movie, and went to go watch that instead of sitting with this endless criticism. He came out in a much better mood and no longer spiraling into a depressive episode. He notes that this same strategy worked in future situations as well. "The next time I started to go down, I remembered that 'Don't I have anything better to do?' I started to laugh. I immediately changed, just went and did something else… It was a choice… After a number of times, not too many, I never got depressed again because this made a habit that if I would start in that direction, the habit was, 'Go do something else.'"

In addition to his negative self-talk and depressive episodes, Bruce also applied this reprogramming to improve his relationships. He had previously been unable to maintain a successful romantic relationship. Why? "I was programmed about relationships by observing my father and my mother. Well, they had dysfunctional relationships. So, what do you think? I downloaded dysfunction," he explains. He found that the root of these issues was his inability to love himself, which meant that in relationships he was projecting the belief that he was unlovable, which inevitably pushed away his partners. But by reprogramming his brain by interrupting the "I am unlovable" program and focusing on loving himself first, he was able to change his behavior in relationships and has now been in a happy relationship with his partner for over 20 years.

So how can this reprogramming be applied in your own life? It is not a matter of just trying harder and thinking positively. Remember, the conscious mind is only active 5% of the time, so even if you direct the conscious mind toward healthier behaviors, the subconscious programs will still win out if new programs aren't instituted. And the worst part is that since the subconscious mind only takes over when you aren't paying attention, you won't even be able to see why your conscious actions aren't resulting in you achieving your goals, and you will just become increasingly frustrated. Therefore, the first step is to begin to notice the programs at play in your own subconscious mind.

The best way to determine what programs are directing you right now is to look around at your life. Look around the room you are sitting in right now. Since your subconscious mind is executing programs on autopilot 95% of the time, your life is a result of the patterns and habits your subconscious has developed and implemented. Noticing the patterns in your life—whether it's an inability to develop and maintain relationships, difficulty believing in yourself, or a fear of taking your business to the next level—will tell you what programs are pushing you currently and what new programs need to be implemented.

Once you begin to notice these programs, the next step is to interrupt them and replace them with new habits. This strategy is also a core fixture of cognitive behavioral therapy, and as such is widely recognized by mental health professionals as a very effective remedy to these negative scripts and patterns. A 2012 journal article entitled "Making health habitual: the psychology of 'habit-formation' and general practice" published in the *British Journal of General Practice* explains, "Within psychology, 'habits' are defined as actions that are triggered automatically in response to contextual cues that have been associated with their performance," and goes on to give the examples of washing your hands after using the restroom or putting on your seatbelt after getting in the car. In other words, a habit becoming automatic isn't just about doing something repeatedly, but about doing something in response to a specific trigger event. In Bruce's examples, the cue was negative self-talk and/or the beginning of a depressive episode. This is why noticing these programs is so important; once you begin to notice and interrupt them, you can form habits around mitigating them, which will eventually become automatic. Throughout this book I've been a proponent of hiring coaches. An intuition coach or mental health therapist or spiritual coach can also help you dig deep into uncovering these patterns and programs.

To apply this in your own life, begin to identify the subconscious patterns guiding you, notice when they kick in, and interrupt them as quickly as possible to replace them with a positive habit. For example, if you find that you have a pattern of letting your perfectionism get in the way of seizing business opportunities, you can begin to notice when these instances occur and immediately respond by throwing yourself into the opportunity, even if you are worried you may not be perfectly ready for it. Another technique is to pay close attention to the predominant question or questions you ask yourself every day. If you are constantly going back over interactions you have with people throughout the course of your day and asking yourself, "How did I come across to that person I just talked to?" or "Was I polite to that person?" then those questions can be the beginning of you discovering the subconscious programming that is guiding your daily life. Maybe you think too much about people's opinions of you. Maybe you are too worried about how people perceive you. Whatever those dominant questions are that you ask yourself everyday can be a great place to start in identifying your subconscious programming.

Finally, the most important program to instill in your subconscious is that of loving yourself, and this program is sadly one of the rarest. Dr. Lipton describes his experience of testing audiences at his talks on this belief. His research has found that over 80% of every audience will not test positive for, "I love myself." Once you are able to instill this belief in yourself, the rest of your habits will evolve to support this belief and help you create your best life. Once you believe you are capable and competent and deserve love and success, your tendency to self-sabotage will fall away and your conscious and subconscious minds will be in harmony. From there, nothing can stop you. This is particularly valuable for those of us who have business ideas that are atypical or challenge the norm. We need to have a subconscious programming that helps us level up in spite of the people who will call our ideas crazy.

3 Laws of Pro Motion

Thinking about your brand building as a form of programming can be instructive. I've developed these brand building frameworks and exercises to help demystify branding and marketing. These exercises are for brand development and marketing using Newton's three laws of motion. Newton's laws of motion are three physical laws that form the basis for classical mechanics. They describe the relationship between a body and the forces acting upon it, its motion, and the forces exerted by one body on another. The first law states that a body will remain at rest or in uniform motion in a straight line unless acted upon by an external force. The second law states that when a force acts on a body, it will cause an acceleration proportional to the magnitude of the force and inversely proportional to the mass of the body. The third law states that when two bodies interact, they exert equal and opposite forces on each other. The following table (Figure 1), Omíládé's laws of pro motion, expands on Newton's laws of motion to demonstrate the force and power of your brand and brand creation.

Newton's Laws of Motion	Omílàdé's Laws of Pro Motion
Every object in a state of uniform motion tends to remain in that state of motion unless an external force is applied to it.	Your brand, in its current state of progress will progress at the same rate unless it experiences a force.
$Force(F) = Mass(M) \times Acceleration(A)$	$Impact(I) = FIST \times POWER$
For every action there is an equal and opposite reaction.	Every move matters! Every bit of promotion will result in some reaction.

Figure 1

Stop viewing branding as daunting. You can think about your branding in terms of physical laws. Following these laws of pro motion and branding is one of the easiest business ideas. Whether we know it or not we are constantly training the world around us on how we think and want to be treated. The difference in personal branding and business branding is that business owners tend to live vicariously through their brands. With this it seems like the brand is an entirely different challenge from just being yourself on a daily basis. However, it's not! The simple definition of "branding" is a mark or impression. Your presence in any space has the potential to leave a mark. The world is a snow globe, and you have the open space to make as many snow angels, snow people, snowball fights, and/or avalanches as you want! As stated in the laws of pro motion, your brand, in its current state of progress, will progress at the same rate unless it experiences a force. Once your brand interacts with media coverage, visibility, networking, social capital, and all of the things discussed in this book, it progresses. When thinking about what you want that brand to be and stand for, ask yourself, *What's my story?*

Everyone has a story. You were born, lived somewhere, and you're here reading this from some space in the world. Story creation is inevitable. Your brand was birthed and is living its life the way you taught it to. The world is experiencing your brand the way you told them to—again, the external forces. However, you have the power to rewrite the narrative or throw in a plot twist whenever you like. Consider the following brand story elements as you build, engage, and publicize:

Brand story elements
- Environment;
- Players;
- Plot;
- Conflict;
- Never ending.

Let's dig deeper into the first law, which is "Every object in a state of uniform motion tends to remain in that state of motion unless an external force is applied to it." My first law states, "Your brand's current state of motion will remain the same unless an external force is applied." The first law of motion (all three laws really) is inherent. We know that we will continue walking at the same pace unless something forces us to run. We unconsciously factor weight, speed, and force into our daily interaction with objects. When creating or shifting your brand story you should evaluate the brand environment first. The second law states, "The relationship between an object's mass m, its acceleration a, and the applied force F is $F = ma$. Acceleration and force are vectors (as indicated by their symbols being displayed in slant bold font); in this law the direction of the force vector is the same as the direction of the acceleration vector." Breaking down the second law of pro motion according to Newton's formula means that the relationship between your brand b, it's growth g, and the applied push P is $P = bg$. Basically, the evidence of the push is the growth; however, the growth is only as big as the push. The push is related to the beginning of growth but is not necessarily related to the continuity of your growth. Finally, Newton's third law states, "For every action there is an equal and opposite reaction." Therefore, in terms of your brand, every bit of promotion will result in some reaction. The reaction is never really negative, it either meets your goals or not. I need you to think strategically about creating, seeking, and landing media opportunities. Promotion is the act of making something more well-known. It can be done through advertising, public relations, or word of mouth. Promotion is a key part of marketing because it helps to make a product or service more visible to potential customers. Promotion can be done through advertising, public relations, or word of mouth. Far too many small business owners are solely focused on business operations, and so they neglect the promotion piece. This is a mistake. Promotion is important for a business because it helps the company reach out to new customers and increase sales. It also helps the company maintain its current customer base by reminding them of the products and services that they offer. Therefore, branding is a lot deeper than creating brand statements that sit on your hard drive. The brand statement and your philosophy behind it is actually integral to the success of your business. The branding exercises below require coaching as a companion. You may or may not feel as if you can afford a coach depending on where you are in your entrepreneurship journey. I've been there and ultimately, as discussed in this book, I had to spend money on coaches when I did not have it in order to level up my business. I know what some of you might be thinking. There are many reasons why people don't want to spend money on a business coach. Some of them are: you think that you can do it on your own, you don't want to admit that you need help, you simply don't have the money for it, or you're even afraid of what your friends and family will say about it.

Oprah Winfrey is a well-known American media proprietor, talk show host, actress, producer, and philanthropist. She has been ranked the richest African American of the 20th century and the greatest Black philanthropist in American history. Oprah often talks about the importance of her coaches along her journey. In particular, Oprah has spoken publicly about spiritual coaches. Oprah has been using spiritual coaches for over 20 years to help her with her own personal growth and development.

Spiritual coaches are people who help you to find your inner voice, your true self, and your life purpose. They can help you to find the answers that you are looking for in life by helping you to connect with your higher self or spirit guides. Anthony O'Neal is the national bestselling author of *Graduate Survival Guide: 5 Mistakes You Can't Afford to Make in College*. He has helped more than a million students make smart decisions with their money, relationships, and education to live a well-balanced life. O'Neal has helped millions of, particularly, Black and Brown people get out of debt so they can start living the life of their dreams through his podcast, *The Table*. O'Neal is vocal about the ways he has been able to experience exponential growth in both his visibility and income through investing in various coaches. As you move through your journey as well as the rest of the tactics and exercises in this book, I cannot stress considering having a coach enough; however, even an accountability partner, mentor, or team members can help you move through these exercises. For the exercises below, feedback/brainstorming sessions should be conducted after each exercise is complete in order to maximize the potential growth of your brand. Do these exercises in the order in which they are presented here.

Branding exercise 1:

Take a week (7 whole days) to observe and take notes on yourself. What are people always saying about you? What are you always saying about you? What do you like? What do you eat? What type of activities do you engage in? The things on this list become the building blocks of your brand and the markets it can extend into. Each of the things you noted are already present in your everyday life. It is important that your brand is not a change of who you are but a total engagement in who you are. This makes for a sustainable branding model. Trying to be something you are not for the sake of getting popular is short-lived. You may make lots of money off it, but in the long run the public will get tired of it (e.g. Nicki Minaj).

Branding exercise 2:

Set branding goals based on the feedback given from exercise 1. Make sure that the goals are a mix of S.M.A.R.T. and large, dreamy, out-of-the box goals. (S.M.A.R.T. = Specific, Measurable, Attainable, Relevant, and Time sensitive.) I recommend three or four SMART goals and two or three dreamy goals. Create a profile of your target audience. Who are they? What do they look like? Where do they shop? What do they eat?

Branding exercise 3:

Take 30 days and just try things! Fully engage in all the things you came up with in exercise 1 purposefully and publicly. Your brand involves people, so it makes no sense to keep it private. Be public and purposeful. Being public can oversaturate the look of the brand with things that don't stick to the psyche of your audience. Being purposeful without being public can stunt the growth of your brand. You are awesome, and everyone should know. Go to your target audience for the purpose of bringing them back to you!

Branding exercise 4:

By the time you get to this exercise you should be well on your way to meeting at least one of your goals. Engaging in everything you've noted thus far has already given your brand a push. Now is the time to take the notes from the last 30 days and throw out what didn't feel comfortable or get any response. Capitalize on what elements of the last 30 days got you the greatest response. Here we will use graphic organizers to draw out the elements that are best for the growth of your brand.

Branding exercise 5:

Check your goals. How close are you to meeting them? Reinvent some aspect of yourself. This exercise never ends. At this point you are at least 60 days into concentrated branding, and the world has changed a few times over. Find the changes in society. Where are you necessary? You are necessary. Be creative. We will brainstorm here and begin exercises 2–5 all over again.

Spending Your Coins

When you are on an upward trajectory in your business where your visibility is increasing and you are making consistent sales, you'll need to be smart about how you spend, invest, and divvy up your income. I find that, even before your business turns a profit you want to put in place good spending habits. Being principled and disciplined when you do not have much money will make it easier to continue following the system when you start making more money. Some advisors will tell you to pay yourself first and then pay the business. There is all types of advice out there, and some of it I find to be from a white patriarchal perspective, quite frankly.

For many years running my businesses, as well as Black Girl Ventures, I didn't have the option to think about the way I spent my money. I just had to survive and do my best to keep the business up and running. When people say things like "Put this amount over here, and put this amount over there" it immediately triggers systematic oppression for me. That advice is assuming you have more than you need. It assumes your business is making a profit. Many Black and Brown businesses are not. The question is literally, do I have enough money to continue buying product? Or paying the minimum on my business credit line? There may not be anything to skim off the top for paying yourself. For a very long time, I had no money to be putting anywhere but back into the business to keep it going. Therefore, I am always cognizant of meeting people where they are at in terms of their individual business, so I do not like to give blanket money advice in that way. I want to be nuanced and not start from a place of privilege. Therefore, my advice is to read your own bookkeeping, to start. Personally, I didn't have money in reserves for more than half the life of my business. I felt when I did have some profit I had to think about reserves. The first thing we typically do when we think about our first experience with profit is to think about spending it. I, however, did not do that. A wealth manager once told me that in life, you have spenders and you have savers. The spenders will spend no matter what. I've seen billionaires spend themselves out of cash because they're just spending. I've seen people who you would consider having no money save enough to become millionaires later in life.

The thing about spending and saving is to get smart around understanding that your savings can be considered a spend. So if saving is a line item that you consider an expense and you invest that savings over a period of time, then you can become very, very wealthy. In essence, you're spending money on yourself, by treating savings as a spend item. This is a powerful perception shift. I am always trying to figure out how I can multiply what is in my cup. This is a great way to do that. Make that small mindset shift first, and then once your business is increasingly becoming profitable, you want to let go of romanticized notions of the income you can actually pay yourself. The pressure to "pay yourself first" too often makes small business owners feel as though they should somehow be paying themselves large salaries. The income you pay yourself may start out as small as $100 dollars or $1,000 dollars a month. It is whatever your business at its current state can provide. This is called taking your owner's draw. And again, this happens after the survival mode phase of your business, where you are just spending your money on keeping the lights on. Your initial goal might be to get to a point where you can pay yourself a small payment. Again, this is very important. There is no reason why you should put pressure on yourself to take a large sum of capital from your business each month, before the business can handle it. Early on be honest with yourself and operate based on what your business can handle. Baby steps are key. In addition, do not be afraid to work day jobs while you build your business to a place where you can pay yourself a salary that allows you to leave that day job. As you've already read, I've had several day jobs along the way, many of which I worked while running my businesses for several years. The apps, such as Task Rabbit and others, make it very easy to bring in income on the side while you build a profitable business. Do not be ashamed or afraid to utilize those things. You can use all types of resources to keep yourself afloat. It's okay to support yourself in other ways, until you can pay yourself a salary.

Hiring Smart

I view hiring as a reinvestment tool. Black Girl Ventures is here to empower women in their journey to becoming successful business owners. Part of the reinvest strategy is not just supporting these women in terms of access to capital but also thinking about the way I hire employees as a reinvestment tool. I view hiring as a tool to reinvest back into the communities that the company serves. I believe that entrepreneurs should consider this when making their first hire, regardless of whether their business is built to particularly serve these communities. Black and Brown business owners, as a collective, can be a force of great financial empowerment and community capital, if they make a concerted effort to hire people of color and women. Of course, white business owners should make a commitment to this as well, but even the early-stage entrepreneur should, where possible, make a commitment to this. There is some interesting research around hiring women that speaks to the bottom line of a company as well. The importance of hiring women is not just about fairness. It's about the bottom line. Women are more likely to be engaged in their work, and they're more likely to stay with a company for a longer period of time. In fact, research has shown that companies with women in leadership are 15% more profitable than those without it. In addition, the importance of hiring Black people is not just about diversity. It's about the bottom line. In a recent study, it was found that companies with more diverse workforces are more likely to have higher returns on equity, better customer satisfaction, and higher employee productivity. Hiring Black people is not just a moral obligation, it's also an economic one.

A number of Black Americans are not part of the labor force, and some hold that this is due to socioeconomic barriers. Black people, who represent 13.6 percent of the total US population, make up about 12 percent of the workforce. In other words, a large proportion of America's Black population is outside the labor force and therefore not part of the economic activity that is supposed to be driving the economy. For example, 37 percent of African Americans 25–54 years old did not work in 2008. The unemployment rate for African Americans was 10 percent, compared to 5.8 percent for whites. However, African Americans have made progress in overcoming the racial economic divide through education. Therefore, at this moment in time, my mission is to be a contributor to being of service to diversifying my ecosystem in a way that aligns with the mission of Black Girl Ventures. That is, to put money in the pockets of people who represent the communities I serve and to play a role in the economic empowerment of people that look like me. Tools and tactics I use to implement this mission include the use of recruiting sites such as LinkedIn. Black Girl Ventures has specifically used LinkedIn to post job ads, and we have paid to boost those job ads in order to get in front of a greater number of potential employees. LinkedIn is a social networking site that is used for professional networking. It has become the most popular social media platform for recruiters to find and contact potential candidates. LinkedIn recruiting services are a great way to find new talent and connect with them. Outside of hiring, LinkedIn is also an extension of our sales and marketing as I've made professional connections to potential investors via the site as well. The network has over 300 million users and provides a great opportunity to grow your business, both in terms of recruiting and ultimately hiring the right candidate for the job. I've found it very rewarding to start within the Black Girl Ventures community in terms of hiring as well. Of course, reinvesting into my community looks like alerting

Black Girl Venture members to company job opportunities at the outset. The Black Girl Ventures Facebook page has over 4,000 members to date, many of whom have participated in pitch events, our fellowship programs, or used resources we've provided to gain access to capital. When we are hiring we tend to invite those who have engaged with us to apply, including through our mailing list.

Some of you just will not have the funds to hire someone paid. One important aspect of hiring is the belief that we can't hire if our business can't afford it. Many small businesses are struggling to make a profit, but they know they need to hire. Your company grows bigger and stronger when you build your team of employees that can help the company reach their goals.

I am here to tell you that if you need somebody for free, just be straight up. When I needed someone that could write blogs and copy for social media, I put a whole job description out to my community and made it clear that I did not have any capital at the moment. The job was going to be fully volunteer, but I explained that I was looking for a person that could take a ride with me. Two women who have been following Black Girl Ventures online for years ended up working for the company, and they worked for free for a year. I was very honest with them, and I told them straight up if they rocked with me, as soon as I got money, I would pay them. One theme of this book early on was not being afraid to ask for help, and this is another one of those examples.

One of the questions I get asked often is what is the first hire a business owner should make. The answer to this question is that it depends. I know this is not as direct as some would like it, but that is truly the answer. It not only depends on the business, but it also depends on your personality as a business owner. For example, if you're not a salesperson, one of your first hires may be a salesperson. However, someone who is already strong in that area will need to bring someone else on as their first hire. Okay. If your business includes lots of creativity on your part and you're not a person that enjoys doing day-to-day KPIs and tracking, then an admin or virtual assistant is who you will need to hire first so that you can be free to create.

In terms of figuring out whom you need to hire first, which is often the real question early-stage entrepreneurs need to clarify, I'd suggest the following steps. The first step is to figure out what you need. Do you need someone who can write content for your website? Do you need someone who can write copy for your social media posts? Do you need someone who can do both? Next, figure out what skills are needed. If you're looking for a content writer, do they need experience in writing blog posts or articles? If you're looking for a copywriter, do they need experience in writing ads or marketing materials? Finally, figure out how much time and money you have to spend. If the budget is tight and the timeline is short, it might be better to hire one person with both skill sets rather than two people with just one skill set. In terms of steps to making that hire, as already discussed, I suggest the following. The first step is to define what you need in a candidate. Next, you should create an advertisement and post it on various job boards or social media sites starting with your own community members. LinkedIn hiring is a great resource to use. Make visible the idea of reinvesting back into your community through hiring. This includes reaching out to your network of friends and family members for referrals or even as potential hires. Once you have found someone who seems like they would be a good fit, it is important to do an interview with them and ask them questions about their experience and qualifications. As early entrepreneurs, we may be tempted to skip the prescreening and formal interviewing steps, but this is crucial. For one, it is a learning process for you in terms of your hiring and interviewing capabilities. This will become crucial down the line when you make bigger and more important hires that are critical to the success of your business. You do not want to skip steps in this process. If the candidate seems like they would be a good fit, then it is time to make an offer. If not, do not be afraid to continue searching for the right person. Hiring is a time-consuming process. It takes a lot of time and effort to find the right candidate for the job.

In addition, the hiring process doesn't stop when an offer is made; it continues into their first day at work. Your company should provide a well-written and comprehensive onboarding packet so new employees can be successful as soon as they begin their job. This can include information on how to complete tasks, how to use company assets, and what to expect on the first day. This is called onboarding, and I see so many early-stage and even veteran entrepreneurs fail to have systems in place for onboarding. A strong onboarding process helps new employees quickly transition into their roles, feel welcomed into their work environment, connect with other staff members, and be successful as soon as they begin their job. Again, you'll be tempted early on to skip steps to save time, but that could be costly down the line and result in high employee turnover for your business. The more you go through the process as a business owner, the better you get at it. As you go through this process, create a procedure and document your hiring process so that you are not re-creating the process each time you need to bring someone new on. Until your business is at a place where you have a human resources department or someone whose sole job is to hire employees, you will be handling these tasks yourself. Put in the time to do it efficiently and effectively.

I've heard business owners say that you should hire people to do the things you do not want to do. That type of advice is coming from a place of privilege many of us may not have based on where we are in our business. As an entrepreneur that is trying to turn a profit and keep the lights on, you should not be hiring someone as an extension of what you don't like to do. Rather, you should be hiring people based on the skill sets that you lack. There are experts who can do lots of the tasks you are doing better. If it isn't your skill set, then hire the person you need to help your business grow who can do that task better than you. Once your business has grown, you are making a profit and you have built a healthy business, you can certainly hire persons including a personal assistant, a home chef and others that complement your lifestyle. However, these certainly shouldn't be the early hires you are making when your mission is to grow a healthy business that you want to thrive. Hiring is a system. It has a procedure and it has results. If you do not have a system in place, then you do not know how well the system works. You do not know where to make tweaks, and if a candidate fails, you do not have a set of steps to go back to in order to see what can be improved upon in the system. I started this chapter out by talking about the importance of programming and reprogramming. Hiring is no different. Life is about inputs and outputs. You create and code the program, and you reap the benefits (or failures) of the results. The beautiful thing about it all is that you learn valuable insights along the way.

About the Authors

Shelly **Omílàdé Bell,** known as "Omi," is a serial entrepreneur and computer scientist with a background in performance poetry, K-12 education, and IP strategy. She was named one of the Top 100 Powerful Women in Business by *Entrepreneur* magazine, Entrepreneur of the Year by Technically DC, and acknowledged as a Rising Brand Star by Adweek. Omi is the Founder/CEO of Black Girl Ventures (BGV). Omi launched BGV from a living room in a house in Southeast DC to a multimillion-dollar game-changing social impact vehicle by using the power of social capital. BGV has held more than 50 programs and funded over 300 Black/Brown women–owned companies across the US, and directly impacted over 20,000 people across 64 countries. BGV has raised more than $1 million for 600-plus participants. Omi has been featured in *Forbes*, on Yahoo Finance, *Good Morning America, Fox Business*, and more.

BGV funds and scales tech-enabled, revenue-generating businesses (under $1M) founded by people who identify as Black/Brown and woman.

Dr. Sheena C. Howard is a multi-hyphenate writer from Philadelphia. As an award-winning writer, creative entrepreneur, and professor of communication, she helps brands, organizations, celebrities and influencers turn their life experiences into compelling narratives.

Index